CU01024643

Published in 2023 by Welbeck Children's
An Imprint of Welbeck Children's Limited,
part of the Welbeck Publishing Group
Offices in: London - 20 Mortimer Street, London W1T 3JW &
Sydney - Level 17, 207 Kent St, Sydney NSW 2000 Australia

www.welbeckpublishing.com

Design and layout © Welbeck Children's Limited 2023

Text copyright © 2023 Damian Johnson
Illustration © 2023 Laura Greenan

A CIP catalogue record for this book is available
from the British Library.

ISBN: 978 1 78312 942 3

Printed in Dubai

1 3 5 7 9 10 8 6 4 2

Author: Damian Johnson
Illustrator: Laura Greenan
Designer: Charlotte Seymour
Design Manager: Matt Drew
Editor: Stella Caldwell
Senior Commissioning Editor: Suhel Ahmed
Picture Research: Paul Langan
Consultant: Dr Jim Lusted
Production: Arlene Lestrade
Publisher: Jane Harris

MIX
Paper | Supporting
responsible forestry
FSC® C004800
FSC
www.fsc.org

Damian Johnson   Laura Greenan

FOOTBALL'S CHAMPIONS OF CHANGE

An inspiring history of the
anti-racism movement in football

WELBECK

Contents

Foreword

Brian Deane

My name is Brian Deane and I scored the first ever Premier League goal on August 15 1992 playing for Sheffield United against Manchester United. I was really excited to read *Football's Champions of Change* because racism is such a relevant topic in football. The current generation of footballers have been united in spreading the anti-racist message by doings things such as taking the knee and speaking out on social media.

There are so many others from my own era and before who faced their own struggles and played a part in making the game we all love more inclusive.

This book is educational with lots of information about amazing people who fought and continue to fight for change. It would have been great to have more of such stories when I was younger to learn about these heroes.

This is an exhilarating read that gives me hope for the future. We can all take inspiration from those who feature in this book. But there is still plenty to do. I will continue to support campaigns for tougher laws to combat online abuse. I know from my own personal experience the difficulty in getting a job in football management. We need to get more diversity in board rooms and among managers. These are two of the many subjects touched on in *Football's Champions of Change*.

I am not sure where the end goal lies, but we have to keep trying to make football a more welcoming place for people regardless of their colour or background.

Introduction

Troy Townsend

Head of Player Engagement at football's equality and inclusion charity, Kick It Out.

This is a very important book for young people. The horrible abuse suffered by the three England players who missed penalties in the EURO 2020 final just goes to show that the issue of racism in football hasn't gone away.

For more than a decade, I have been fighting the good fight, trying to combat discrimination in all forms within the game. I want to help make it a level playing field with all under-represented groups becoming an accepted part of football.

In the past, players from ethnic minorities suffered direct abuse and there were no consequences for the offenders. I went through that myself, and as a father and a grandfather, I don't want future generations to experience it. Through campaigning, we have now made sure that there are punishments for people who discriminate.

However, racism and discrimination in football and society has not completely gone away. We have made progress, but a lot more needs to be done. There is a new wave of people with hatred in their hearts and minds. We see it expressed in some football grounds, but it mainly appears in social media.

The key is education, and that is a big part of my job at the charity Kick It Out. I constantly go into football club academies to speak to players – from age nine through to 23. We have open group conversations in which they hear their team-mates speak about how racism has affected them. We also talk to parents.

It helps people who have offended to understand the impact of their words and gestures. When you have been targeted because of your colour or race, it damages your mental well-being. It sits in your mind and impacts your life and your family's life.

This book is a very good introduction to many of the important issues about race. It explains why we are where we are and introduces you to some key historical and modern-day figures who have fought for change. Of course, it can't cover everything, but hopefully it will encourage you to discover more. I hope you enjoy the journey.

1

FOOTBALL UNDER THE SPOTLIGHT

Since the earliest days of British football, there have been players from ethnic minority backgrounds in the game. Although supporters hailed many as heroes for their achievements on and off the pitch, the same figures also endured racial abuse and discrimination purely on grounds of their ethnicity.

The tireless work of anti-racist campaigners has helped reduce the worst cases of racial abuse. But a backlash against black players who missed penalties for England in the Euro 2020 final has showed that there is still some way to go in overcoming discrimination.

Our Heroes Stand Tall

On a hot July evening in 2021, families up and down the country sat down to watch England take on Italy in the final of Euro 2020. Fans had waited more than half a century to see their team reach a major final and football fever gripped the nation.

After battling it out for 120 minutes, the two sides were tied and faced each other in a penalty shoot-out. Fans watched nervously – everyone knew England's terrible record in penalty shoot-outs, but desperately hoped this time the team could win.

Among the brave penalty takers were three black players, **Marcus Rashford**, **Bukayo Saka** and **Jadon Sancho**. Sadly, all three missed – and a tournament that had brought the country together ended in heartbreak.

Rashford, Saka and Sancho had been inspirational in helping their team reach the final, but now they were subjected to a torrent of hateful racist abuse. Some online abusers posted emojis of monkeys and bananas, a disgusting insult suggesting black people are closer to animals than to humans.

...ruined it for us.

Get out of my country!

Watching England reach the final showed us how football can be a force for good. The team's success inspired feelings of joy and togetherness, but the manner of their defeat also revealed deep-seated racist attitudes in a minority of the population.

Before the tournament started, the England players insisted on 'taking the knee' – an anti-racist gesture that originated in 2013 from the Black Lives Matter movement (see page 117) in the United States.

> **❝** *I can take critique of my performance all day long... but I will never apologise for who I am and where I came from.* **❞**
>
> Marcus Rashford

WALL OF HONOUR

Striker **Marcus Rashford** has a mural in his home city of Manchester, a tribute to his work campaigning against racism and on behalf of underprivileged children. Sickeningly, it was vandalised after his penalty miss. However, the haters didn't have the final word – hundreds of people left heart-warming messages of support on the artwork, and well-known public figures also leapt to the defence of the England players.

> **❝** *The reaction of the England players following the racist abuse has been measured, intelligent and dignified. These young men are a fine example to all of us. Proud of each and every one of them.* **❞**
>
> Gary Lineker – **Match Of The Day** presenter

By continuing to speak out against racism, the England team – backed by their manager Gareth Southgate – became standard-bearers in British sport for the fight against discrimination.

> **❝** *By reporting these comments to the police, by driving out the hate and being kind to one another, we will win. Love always wins.* **❞**
>
> Bukayo Saka

The Football Revolution

In 1992, the creation of the English Premier League kicked off a revolution in English football. Before then, the top clubs played in the first division of the Football League. Grounds were often shabby and even unsafe, while fan violence was a constant threat and racial abuse on the terraces aimed at black players was commonplace.

The clubs in the newly formed Premier League attracted the most fans and brought in money from TV revenue. This newfound wealth drew the best players, while government grants funded stadium renovations, and as hooligans were driven out, campaigns to stamp out racism began to take off.

Players from ethnic minority backgrounds had gradually been increasing in the old first division. But now, as players from across the globe flocked to join the Premier League, their numbers soared. Other leagues couldn't compete financially, so they mainly recruited players from their own countries. England, with its strong international links and big salaries, was the place to be for players from across the world.

Although the English game has always been popular with fans overseas, the Premier League increased that appeal. Viewers are drawn by its diversity as well as the quality of the football. Players from more than a hundred nations have taken part, and the number of British ethnic minority players has also risen consistently with each passing season. With more than 200 countries broadcasting the matches, the Premier League has the largest television audience in the world, which helps to make it the richest football league in the world.

War on racism

Despite all the progress made in the past 30 years, the shadow of racism sadly continues to loom over the game. Shockingly, there has been a 50 per cent rise in football-related racist incidents reported to the police in England and Wales in recent years. The Premier League itself has encouraged supporters to report incidents to the police, joining forces with organisations such as The Football Association (The FA), Kick It Out, Show Racism The Red Card, and The Professional Footballers' Association (PFA). Together, they help to educate young people about the importance of diversity and the need to speak out when confronted with prejudice.

The creation of the Premier League has concentrated money and power in the hands of the top clubs, which many believe is unfair. But to their credit, clubs such as Manchester City, Manchester United and Liverpool have used their power and influence to help fight discrimination. Many ethnic minority players have achieved their footballing ambitions and become role models in the fight against racism.

GAME CHANGERS !!

French striker **Thierry Henry,** of Caribbean descent, was an Arsenal star between 1999 and 2007. The team went an entire league season undefeated in 2003/04 and earned the name The Invincibles.

South Korean midfielder **Park Ji Sung** joined Manchester United in 2005 and was the first Asian player to win the Champions League in 2008. He endured racial chants from the terraces, but rose above them to deliver some stellar performances.

"I'M JUST A NORMAL LAD FROM LIVERPOOL WHOSE DREAM HAS JUST COME TRUE"

Defender **Trent Alexander-Arnold** had won both the Premier League (2022) and Champions League (2019) with Liverpool by the time he was 21. He is a powerful symbol for the city's large black community, which is the oldest in Britain.

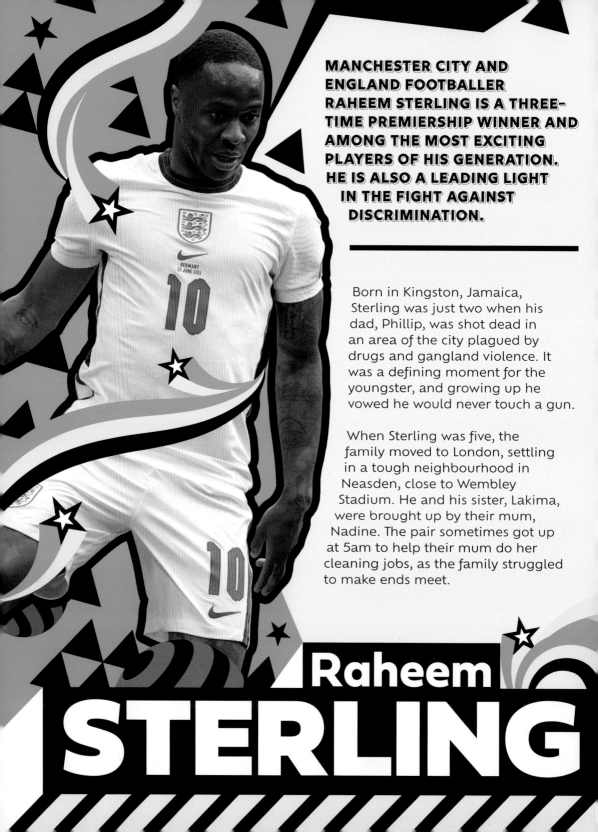

MANCHESTER CITY AND ENGLAND FOOTBALLER RAHEEM STERLING IS A THREE-TIME PREMIERSHIP WINNER AND AMONG THE MOST EXCITING PLAYERS OF HIS GENERATION. HE IS ALSO A LEADING LIGHT IN THE FIGHT AGAINST DISCRIMINATION.

Born in Kingston, Jamaica, Sterling was just two when his dad, Phillip, was shot dead in an area of the city plagued by drugs and gangland violence. It was a defining moment for the youngster, and growing up he vowed he would never touch a gun.

When Sterling was five, the family moved to London, settling in a tough neighbourhood in Neasden, close to Wembley Stadium. He and his sister, Lakima, were brought up by their mum, Nadine. The pair sometimes got up at 5am to help their mum do her cleaning jobs, as the family struggled to make ends meet.

Raheem
STERLING

However, despite his success on the pitch, Sterling himself became a target for abuse – regardless, he grew increasingly confident in speaking out on issues of discrimination.

In 2017, he was attacked outside Manchester City's training ground by a man who was jailed for racially aggravated assault. The following year, Chelsea banned six spectators for using racist language and threatening behaviour towards the player during a Premier League match.

Sterling often got into trouble at school, but he loved playing football. His speed and skill on the ball attracted attention, and he joined the academy at Queens Park Rangers Football Club when he was still at primary school. At the age of 15, Sterling was signed by Liverpool, and he left north London for Merseyside. It was there that he remembers encountering racism. On one occasion, he was recognised in the street by a stranger, racially abused and headbutted in an unprovoked assault.

The abuse didn't deter the teenager, though. After making the first team at Liverpool, he earned his first England cap at 17 and played in the 2014 FIFA World Cup in Brazil. His performances would lead to a £49 million move to Manchester City the following year, where his star quality helped the team become a top side. In 2019, the club won a domestic treble: the Premier League, the FA Cup and the League Cup.

Sterling has also accused tabloid newspapers of encouraging racism. For example, in some articles they have criticised black players while celebrating their white team-mates for the same actions, such as buying expensive gifts for his friends and family. Sterling has emerged as a powerful voice in the support of the Black Lives Matter movement and the United Nations' Fight Racism campaign.

In 2021, he launched his own foundation to offer financial support to schools and disadvantaged youngsters in Jamaica and the UK. He often visits his old school in North London, where he is seen as a role model to many of the kids.

In 2021, Sterling was awarded the MBE in the Queen's Birthday Honours List for services to racial equality.

What Is Racism?

Football is played around the world, drawing millions of fans. While the team sport brings a lot of joy to spectators, players from ethnic minority backgrounds sometimes fall victim to racial discrimination, both on and off the pitch. **But what is racism?**

No two people are exactly the same, but we can be grouped together with others who share physical characteristics, nationality, beliefs, language and the same way of life. Many differences between groups are obvious, such as skin colour, hair and features. Others are less clear – religion and culture, for example. All of them, however, help to define a racial or ethnic group.

Racism is when people of a particular ethnicity falsely believe that people of a different group are inferior to them. They judge and mistreat others based on that belief. At its most extreme, this mistreatment might take the form of physical violence, threats of violence, and verbal or written abuse. It might be unjust treatment based on a person's race by an individual or organisation.

Racism can also be more subtle, such as stereotyping – believing that all people with particular racial characteristics are the same, for example. People can stereotype others of a different race without even realising it. This is known as **unconscious bias**. It happens when we judge people based on deeply ingrained attitudes from our background that we are not aware of.

> **"** I don't see colour. It's different now. Not as bad as in the past. **"**

> **"** Sometimes racism is felt, not just through words but through actions, the way people look at you as well. **"**

18

Origins of racism

Although the debate is ongoing, some historians have traced back the idea that humanity can be divided into superior and inferior groups to the attitudes of the ancient Greeks to their Persian enemies. Thereafter, such attitudes were adopted, tweaked and reformulated by Europeans, particularly from the late 17th century, as some countries extended their power and influence by building overseas empires.

European powers often used religion and 'science' (see page 29) to justify colonising another country, claiming the need to make the native population more 'civilised'. For example, this was the attitude that gave rise to the British Empire, which once controlled nearly a quarter of the world's population.

What's more, it was from the early 1500s that European ship captains bought enslaved people from African traders, took them across the Atlantic – to Brazil or a Caribbean island – and forced them into slavery. It wasn't until the 1700s that some people in Great Britain came to think that slavery was wrong.

There are many examples of successful campaigns against racism. The abolitionist movement helped to end slavery in Europe and America in the 19th century. In South Africa, the dismantling of apartheid – which forced non-whites to live separate lives – took decades of activism before culminating between 1990 and 1994.

Frederick Douglass *(1817–95)* was an African-American diplomat, abolitionist and writer.

He had an ability to rouse people with his brilliant speeches and became leader of the movement to abolish slavery in the United States. Douglass was once enslaved himself. Throughout his life, together with his wife and family, he fought for racial justice and equality.

Racism's ugly face in football

Although progress has been made over the years, racism in football continues to be a problem today. With players from ethnic minority backgrounds the primary target, abuse from fans, or between players from opposing teams, is the most visible form. It might occur when a particular player scores or misses a shot, or even touches the ball.

In this age of the internet, racist comments are often voiced on social media after a match, perhaps because by using this platform abusers can remain anonymous. A recent report found that in 2020 alone nearly 3,000 abusive messages were posted, and more than half of those messages contained some form of racial harassment.

The good news is that many in the game, including high-profile players and former players, are at the forefront of the battle to eradicate racism. Campaigns, such as the Premier League's No Room for Racism and the charity Kick It Out (see pages 76–77) have dedicated resources to educating others on the racism issues in football.

Oi, @€*%!

" The reality of racism in sport is the reality of racism in society. "

Herman Ousley from Kick It Out to the Institute of Race Relations, 2011

You ¥©¢#!

We hate your kind!

Italy's **Mario Balotelli** has often responded to racist chants by raising his performance on the pitch.

This iconic photo of Liverpool's **John Barnes** in 1988 captures the abuse the former England star faced during his career. Barnes is photographed casually back-heeling a banana thrown at him by someone in the crowd at Everton. At the time, Barnes was among the best players in the world. His reaction reveals his contempt for his abuser even though Barnes claims not to remember the incident as things like this "happened all the time". It came at the end of a dark decade for football but heralded the start of a new era that saw concerted attempts to rid the game of racial abuse.

66 *Any discrimination towards any footballer is a very small, minute part of racial discrimination towards black people.* 99

John Barnes

Racist Incidents In British Football

This timeline highlights significant examples of recorded incidents of racism in football throughout history. It is not a comprehensive list but rather a snapshot to show that the problem is deep-rooted and has existed for decades.

1925

Jack Leslie (see pages 44-45) is the first black player named in an England squad. The invitation is withdrawn when The FA discovers his colour.

1938

Everton's legendary white striker, **Dixie Dean**, punches a spectator who calls him a *"black b#####d"* and is congratulated for his actions by a watching policeman.

1940s

Jamaican **Lindy Delapenha** is the first black player to win the first division at Portsmouth before becoming a top goal scorer for Middlesbrough. He laughs in the faces of abusive fans.

1988

An iconic photo captures Liverpool's **John Barnes** back-heeling a banana thrown at him during a match at Everton (see page 21).

1995

Eric Cantona, of Manchester United, launches himself at a Crystal Palace supporter hurling racist abuse from the crowd.

1885

Scotland's first black international, **Andrew Watson**, is subjected to "vulgar insults by splenetic, ill-tempered players".

1887

Britain's first black professional footballer, **Arthur Wharton** (p.32–33), is described as "a darkie" and not fit to play for England by the *Athletic Journal*.

1909

The *London Football Star* is the first publication to mention racial abuse against Spurs' Walter Tull: "A section of the crowd made a cowardly attack in language lower than Billingsgate [a fish market]".

1965

Albert Johanneson (p.48–49) is the first player of African heritage to play in an FA Cup final. His career with Leeds Utd is cut short after constant abuse from the terraces destroys his confidence.

1970s

Anti-semetic chants are heard from opposition fans taunting Tottenham FC and their historic links to the Jewish community.

1982

West Bromwich Albion striker **Cyrille Regis** receives a threatening letter containing a bullet on the eve of his England debut.

2004

Football pundit Ron Atkinson is sacked by ITV after a microphone picks up his racist comments about Chelsea player **Marcel Desailly**.

2017

Four Chelsea fans are convicted after pushing a black commuter off a Paris Metro train while chanting *"We're racist and that's the way we like it"*.

2021

England players **Marcus Rashford**, **Bukayo Saka** and **Jadon Sancho** draw universal praise for a dignified and united response to hateful abuse on social media after missing penalties at Euro 2020.

Why I'm A...
CHAMPION
OF CHANGE

Name: Tino Daishe

Age: 12

Favourite Footballer:
Paul Gascoigne

My mum and dad are from Zimbabwe. I was born in a city called Bulawayo but moved to the UK six years ago. I play on the right wing, and I look up to Lionel Messi and Cristiano Ronaldo because of their skill and work ethic.

At school, if people ever make fun of me because of my colour, I go home and tell my parents, who inform the teachers at school. I have received a few racist comments while playing football too, such as "You're black so you can't play football" and "Tino, you're too black. Your skin is too dark." I used to get it quite a lot and it hurt. It really upset me. I managed to deal with it by telling the coaches.

I have started to open up and tell people how I am feeling. I speak to my parents, my uncle and my coaches about what has been going on. It has pretty much stopped now.

I think there are a lot of organisations who are trying their best to stop racism in football. As time goes on, the situation will improve. Of course, racism will never stop completely, but these organisations will keep working until it happens a lot less. Hopefully, I am going to be a professional footballer. My dream is to play for Chelsea. Will I play for England or Zimbabwe? I choose England. Unfortunately, the situation in Zimbabwe is bad at the moment.

Your skin is too dark.

When I see players from different backgrounds playing in English football it makes me feel more welcome. If you hear people saying "He's black. He's not going to make it in football", it's really upsetting. When you see people from other backgrounds playing football it makes you happier and more determined to succeed.

He's black. He's not going to make it in football.

Tino, you're too black. Your skin is too dark.

2

BACK IN THE DAY...

Football, as we know it, was born in an era we would hardly recognise today.

It was the 19th century. Britain, with a huge empire stretching across the globe, was the richest country on earth. Slavery had a significant but shameful role in creating the nation's wealth and helped shape white people's attitudes towards people of other races, who were widely considered as inferior.

Attitudes Of Empire

Throughout the 18th century Britain became more industrialised and required materials for its booming manufacturing economy. Backed by the government, which had already been growing its empire for almost 200 years, industrialists travelled overseas and established more colonies in Africa, Asia and the Americas, shipping valuable resources back to the motherland.

Often, the colonisers used violence and oppression to maintain control, many justifying their actions with the 'moral' belief that they were on a mission to 'civilise' the indigenous population.

Some were paternalists who thought they could teach the native population how to run their own countries. Others believed the non-white people were incapable of self-governance.

Racist opinions in Britain hardened even further as missionaries found it harder to convert local populations to Christianity. The sense of superiority increased with many newspaper stories describing heroic deeds in capturing and controlling new territories. Most British people at the time believed the British Empire – the largest of its kind in history – was a force for good and rarely saw inhabitants of foreign colonies as equals.

The empire developed trade in these new lands, albeit acting in its own economic interests, and spread Christian values. The Victorian writer Rudyard Kipling spoke of the "white man's burden" to describe what was then seen as Britain's duty to advance under-developed parts of the world.

Hostile greeting

When Queen Victoria took the throne in 1837, Britain was the world's most technologically advanced nation and the dominant global military power. By this time, pressed by ethical concerns, Britain had committed to end its slave trade globally. However, the attitudes towards people of other races had already become ingrained in some quarters of the national psyche.

At the time, most migration to Britain was predominantly from Europe, especially Ireland. Jewish people arrived in large numbers to escape persecution in Russia. There was also a flux of Africans who had been freed in British colonies after the abolition of slavery in Britain in 1833. The new arrivals were accepted by some, but many others were openly hostile to them. It was into this environment that football was born.

Jean Louis Rodolphe Agassiz *(1807–73)* was a Swiss-born American biologist and geologist.

He was a keen advocate for polygenism and used the theory to argue that black people were an inferior race. His views are said to have encouraged the trading of slaves.

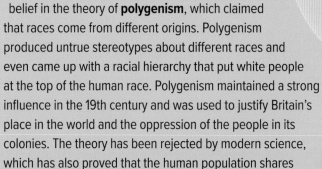

FAKE SCIENCE

In the Victorian era, there was widespread belief in the theory of **polygenism**, which claimed that races come from different origins. Polygenism produced untrue stereotypes about different races and even came up with a racial hierarchy that put white people at the top of the human race. Polygenism maintained a strong influence in the 19th century and was used to justify Britain's place in the world and the oppression of the people in its colonies. The theory has been rejected by modern science, which has also proved that the human population shares 99 per cent of its DNA and biological differences are minimal.

Football's
Working-Class Roots

In the mid-18th century, the Industrial Revolution in Britain saw materials flow in from the colonies to the large factories built in the towns and ports. This encouraged millions of people to flock to these big urban centres in search of work.

Factory workers were generally among the poorest in society and at the bottom of the class structure. What's more, the working conditions in factories were often unpleasant and the hours long – typically ten to 12 hours a day. To escape these harsh realities, workers sought leisure activities to enjoy during their free time. In the mid-19th century, the main pastime sports were horse racing, cricket, athletics and boxing, but football was growing in popularity.

The game grew in Britain's manufacturing epicentres in the midlands and north-west, with these regions soon becoming the nation's footballing homeland. Some of the UK's most successful football clubs were the product of industrial communities,

such as Manchester, Liverpool, Sheffield, Glasgow and Newcastle, with some formed from work teams. Huge stadiums were built to fit an overwhelmingly working-class fan base – each with a strong local identity – giving rise to boisterous tribal behaviour (see page 41).

By the 1880s, the practice of pitch invasions had become common in British football, as had more malicious incidents of player abuse and post-game brawling between rival spectators, especially in the north. In an overwhelmingly white society, the football grounds were also an environment where, sadly, 'difference' was often met with suspicion, hostility and abuse.

RULES OF THE GAME

The majority of the men who met at the Freemason's Arms in west London in 1863 to agree a set of laws for football were from English public schools. The modern game they helped create, though, appealed mainly to working-class communities.

> 66 ...in its primitive form football primarily belonged to the lowest level of society. 99
>
> Jim Keoghan, football writer

TARTAN TRAILBLAZER

When the first black players began to appear in Britain, offensive language was routinely used to describe them. **John Walker** was the first black man to play in both the Scottish and English leagues – standing out as a speedy, skilful winger for Hearts in Scotland and Lincoln City in England's second division. It was his colour that attracted the most attention. One newspaper previewed his debut for Leith Athletic in 1898:

> 66 Walker is a coloured player from Leith Primrose of no little repute. He is the first 'darkie' to become a Scottish League player and his appearance is certain to cause no little interest. 99
>
> Scottish referee, 11 March 1898

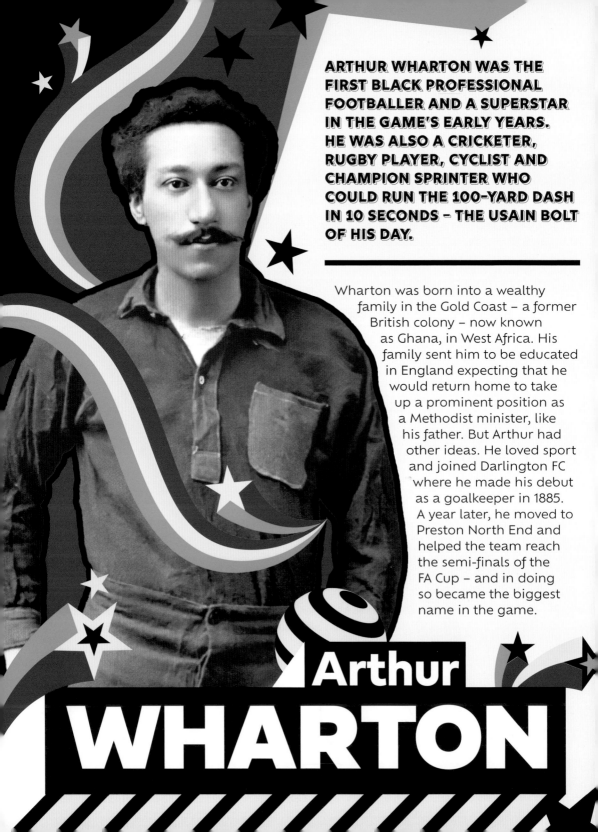

ARTHUR WHARTON WAS THE FIRST BLACK PROFESSIONAL FOOTBALLER AND A SUPERSTAR IN THE GAME'S EARLY YEARS. HE WAS ALSO A CRICKETER, RUGBY PLAYER, CYCLIST AND CHAMPION SPRINTER WHO COULD RUN THE 100-YARD DASH IN 10 SECONDS – THE USAIN BOLT OF HIS DAY.

Wharton was born into a wealthy family in the Gold Coast – a former British colony – now known as Ghana, in West Africa. His family sent him to be educated in England expecting that he would return home to take up a prominent position as a Methodist minister, like his father. But Arthur had other ideas. He loved sport and joined Darlington FC where he made his debut as a goalkeeper in 1885. A year later, he moved to Preston North End and helped the team reach the semi-finals of the FA Cup – and in doing so became the biggest name in the game.

Arthur
WHARTON

Back then, football was violent and goalkeepers were often a target. A natural showman, Wharton had some unorthodox ways to defend himself. He would swing from the crossbar, so attackers were unable to knock him over. Sometimes he caught the ball between his legs or crouched near the post before leaping up to punch it clear.

Despite his talents, Wharton was not spared from racism. For example, at the starting line before a 100-yard race (about 90 metres), he heard two rivals questioning why they had to race a black man. Arthur invited them to fight him, but the pair quickly backed down.

Rising above the prejudice, Wharton turned professional in 1889 with Rotherham Town. His career took him to Sheffield United, Stalybridge Rovers, Ashton North End and Stockport County before he retired in 1902. At the height of his footballing career, there were calls for him to be selected for England. It's believed the Victorian attitudes towards black people meant he was never picked.

Wharton was a trailblazer off the pitch, too. A charitable man, he gave away some of his earnings to the poor. Once Wharton hung up his boots in 1902, he could only find manual work in coal mines and joined the Home Guard of his adopted country when war was declared in 1914. Sadly, he developed a drinking problem in his latter years and died, penniless, in 1930. He was buried in an unmarked grave in Doncaster.

It was the campaigning of Darlington-based artist Shaun Campbell (below), and organisations such as Football Unites Racism Divides that brought Wharton's name back to prominence. A proper headstone was erected at his grave and a statue was erected in 2014 at St George's Park – the home of England's national teams. Wharton finally had his rightful place in history.

> **66** *The world's first black professional footballer was truly ahead of his time and left a fantastic legacy for the generations that have followed him.* **99**
>
> Shaun Campbell, Arthur Wharton Foundation

Artist Shaun Campbell with his mural of Arthur Wharton.
Photo: Stuart Bolton

The Early Barrier Breakers

A handful of players defied the hostile racial attitudes that were so widespread during the earliest days of football. The following pioneers all helped to break down the colour barrier. Their contribution was only fully recognised thanks to the efforts of modern-day historians and campaigners.

Andrew Watson
1856–1921

Andrew Watson was the first British black footballer to play at international level. He captained Scotland in a 6–1 win over England at the Oval cricket ground in 1881 and played his entire career as an amateur. He is recognised as someone who revolutionised the game by teaching his English peers the 'science' of a more dynamic passing style.

Emma Clarke
1876–1905

Hailing from Liverpool, **Emma Clarke** is considered to be the first black female footballer. The early women's game was often described by men as "grotesque". Clarke defied the opposition to join the British Ladies Football Club. Operating mainly as an outfield player, she was once described by the *South Wales Daily News* as "the fleet-footed dark girl on the right wing".

FOOTBALL'S CHAMPIONS OF CHANGE

FOOTBALL'S CHAMPIONS OF CHANGE

Willie Clarke | 1878–1949

Scotland's **Willie Clarke** (no relation to Emma Clarke) was the first black professional footballer to score in the English Football League, playing for Aston Villa in 1901. He spent four years at Villa Park before moving to Bradford City, where he scored the club's first goal in the top division in 1908. Strong and quick, he operated mainly on the right wing, and was once described by the Leeds Mercury as Bradford's "brilliant outside right".

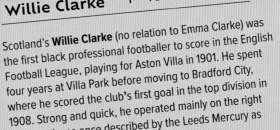

Hassan Hegazi
1889–1961

Known as 'the classy gentleman from Egypt', **Hassan Hegazi** played for Fulham in 1911, scoring in a 3–1 win over Stockport County. As a student, he appeared in the annual match between the universities of Cambridge and Oxford. He also represented his country on the pitch at the 1920 and 1924 Summer Olympic Games.

Walter Tull
1888–1918

Walter Tull survived a tough upbringing to become the first black player in top-flight English football, playing for Tottenham Hotspur. However, he suffered terrible racial abuse from opposition fans. In 1911, he left Spurs for Northampton Town, where he played 111 games. The outbreak of the First World War saw Tull become the first black officer in the British Army, but he was killed in action in 1918.

Why I'm A...
CHAMPION OF CHANGE

Name: Demi Stokes

Age: 30

Favourite footballer: Rachel Yankey

Occupation: Professional footballer

I was born in Birmingham and moved to South Shields when I was three. It was a bit of a culture shock growing up in the area. There were very few mixed-race families on our estate. My mum was white, and my dad Jamaican, and then there was us – three mixed-race kids and my younger brother, who was white.

Getting my hair done was always a bit of an event. I had to wait until the summer holidays for my nan to take us all to Birmingham, where I'd see lots of people who looked like me. These trips have made me realise how important it is to have role models to inspire you.

At home, I got into football. Things weren't great all the time. I played for an all-girls team in an all-boys league. In my first game, when I was eight, I was racially abused. A boy called me the 'P-word'. I thought that's not me because I'm Jamaican but that's the kind of thing ignorant people said in South Shields. I complained to the referee and the boy got taken off.

On the estate, you would experience that kind of thing daily. I wouldn't want anyone to go through it, but I'm grateful for my journey. If I hadn't experienced it, I wouldn't know what I know now.

I idolised Rachel Yankey. For my 15th birthday, I got an England top with Yankey's number

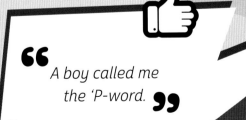

11 on the back. I remember thinking, "Wow, she's good." She played left wing and now I play in the same position. It was the first time I saw someone who looked similar to me playing football, and I wanted to do what she did. I have always looked up to her.

To improve diversity, I think we need to go into youth clubs and inner cities because that's where you'll find talent. If I hadn't been helped by other players' mums and dads, who took me to football, I might have missed out. Some kids can't always get to training or tournaments. We are missing out a lot of talent because of that.

I am grateful to be in the position I'm in. I hope to pass that feeling on to someone else. I hold great responsibility and am making a bigger difference than I thought. I am proud to help.

3

THE RISE IN
TRIBALISM

While football in its primitive form was popularised by the working class in the north, it was the English public schools (a type of fee-charging private school for older boys) that played a big role in the creation of modern football. Playing the game was seen as a character-building pastime for children of the upper classes. It was the ruling class that established the original laws and dominated the early years of organised football.

However, successful new clubs in working-class industrial areas in the north of England challenged the dominance of the public school teams. Their football attracted large crowds of working men, inspired strong emotions and became a source of local pride. Some clubs even paid their players. By 1888, when the Football League was established, the tribal nature of the fan culture we recognise today had taken shape.

Them And Us

Football might have had its roots in the fee-paying public schools, but it was the working classes that turned it into a national spectator sport. The Factory Acts of the 19th century meant shorter hours for workers at weekends. The factory workers of industrial cities, such as Manchester, Sheffield and Nottingham, now had an affordable pastime and flocked to football matches after work.

The teams of the north were often located in the heart of working-class communities, in places such as Bolton, Burnley and Stoke-on-Trent.

The north grabbed the initiative in shaping both the game and fan culture when Blackburn Olympic – a team mainly made up of manual workers from local cotton mills – beat the Old Etonians in the 1883 FA Cup final.

In fact, when the Football League was created in 1888, half of the founding member clubs were from Lancashire. As these clubs were located close to one another, intense local rivalries naturally grew. What's more, the literacy rate among the working class was steadily rising, and young men were reading stories in the newspapers about those rivalries, which captured their imaginations.

Illustrations and club crests from the 1883 FA Cup final between Blackburn Olympic and the Old Etonians at Kennington Oval in London.

Intense battleground

In his 1929 novel, *The Good Companions*, J.B. Priestley described one of his character's feelings of following a fictional team of the 1920s, Bruddersford United F.C.

The novel romanticised the experience, but in reality, the football ground was a harsh, all-male environment. Spectators packed into primitive – and often unsafe – standing areas, creating a rowdy atmosphere in which they were often abusive towards the opposition and people outside of their group.

> **66** ...*you had escaped with most of your mates and your neighbours, with half the town, and there you were, cheering together, thumping one another on the shoulders, swopping judgements like lords of the earth...* **99**
>
> Extract from *The Good Companions*

Players were pelted with stones and bottles, and after matches, fights broke out between opposing fan groups at railway stations. The authorities took a lenient view as long as disturbances did not disrupt matches. Incidents of racial abuse were never challenged.

WHAT IS TRIBALISM?

Tribes are groups of people who share a strong sense of identity that binds them together. This could include where they're from, their language, their beliefs, or even the team they support.

Historically, tribes formed to ensure their survival against hostile outside forces. In modern societies, human beings are still tribal even though we live in a diverse world.

Tribalism allows for a shared expression of love for a football team. It explains why fans remain loyal to their team through thick and thin. But it can also give rise to hostility towards people outside the group, leading to ugly tendencies such as racism.

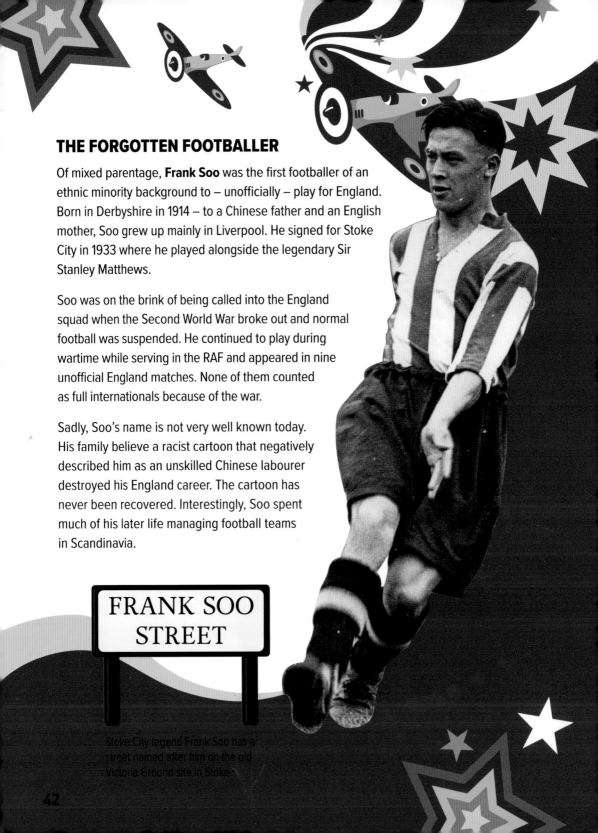

THE FORGOTTEN FOOTBALLER

Of mixed parentage, **Frank Soo** was the first footballer of an ethnic minority background to – unofficially – play for England. Born in Derbyshire in 1914 – to a Chinese father and an English mother, Soo grew up mainly in Liverpool. He signed for Stoke City in 1933 where he played alongside the legendary Sir Stanley Matthews.

Soo was on the brink of being called into the England squad when the Second World War broke out and normal football was suspended. He continued to play during wartime while serving in the RAF and appeared in nine unofficial England matches. None of them counted as full internationals because of the war.

Sadly, Soo's name is not very well known today. His family believe a racist cartoon that negatively described him as an unskilled Chinese labourer destroyed his England career. The cartoon has never been recovered. Interestingly, Soo spent much of his later life managing football teams in Scandinavia.

FRANK SOO
STREET

Stoke City legend Frank Soo has a street named after him on the old Victoria Ground site in Stoke.

The blame game

Very few people from ethnic minority backgrounds lived in Britain in the early 1900s. They were often concentrated in the dockside communities in large cities, such as London, Liverpool and Bristol, which had traded African slaves.

Naturally, there was some integration between people of different ethnic backgrounds. They worked together and got married. All too frequently though, marriage between different races –

especially black men and white women – was condemned by the white majority as a legacy of the ideas of scientific racism (see page 29) that viewed racial groups as being inherently different.

With a shortage of jobs after the First World War, people from these new communities were blamed for denying the white population jobs and housing. It sparked race riots in 1919. The worst of the violence occurred in Liverpool, Cardiff and Newcastle.

There is some evidence that racial tensions in this era spread to football. The British Union of Fascists, a notorious and violent far-right political organisation of the 1930s, exploited these tensions when it tried to recruit football supporters to its cause.

RACISM REPORT

A newspaper called The Football Star may have been the first to report on a racist incident involving Tottenham's **Walter Tull** (see page 35). It published an article titled 'Football and the Colour Prejudice', citing an away match Tull had played in against Bristol City in 1909.

The newspaper was very critical of the way Tull was treated by a section of home fans. "Let me tell those Bristol hooligans that Tull is so clean in mind and method as to be a model for all white men who play football," the report concluded.

AN UNLIKELY TRAILBLAZER, JACK LESLIE WOULD HAVE BEEN THE FIRST PERSON OF COLOUR TO PLAY FOR ENGLAND BUT HIS CALL-UP WAS WITHDRAWN. IT IS WIDELY BELIEVED THAT THIS OCCURRED AFTER THE SELECTORS REALISED HE WAS BLACK.

The son of a Jamaican father and an English mother, Jack Leslie was born in the East End of London in 1901 and began work as a boilermaker.

Leslie moved to Plymouth Argyle in 1921 from his local club, Barking Town, where he had proved himself a prolific goal scorer. Despite the racial attitudes of the day, he quickly became a crowd favourite for Plymouth, who were then in the third tier of English football.

On an autumn day in October 1925, Leslie was called into his manager's office and told the news that he was in the England squad to face Ireland.

Jack
LESLIE

The campaign shares Leslie's story to celebrate diversity and combat racism. Matt Tiller wrote a song in Leslie's honour with the profits going to the campaign.

His selection was widely reported in the press. In those days, the England team was picked by a panel of selectors from the Football Association. It is thought that many of them did not realise the colour of Leslie's skin. When it became clear they dropped him.

Leslie was often described as a quiet and humble gentleman. His reaction to being picked and then dropped by England's selectors typified his character when he spoke about it years later: "They must have forgot I was a coloured boy." He was never selected to play for his country again.

Jack became a legendary figure in Plymouth Argyle's history – scoring 137 goals in his 14 years at the club. Many argue that it is a sign of racism embedded in the way football was run, known as institutional racism, that such an accomplished player had to return to his original trade as a boilermaker after his playing career. Sadly, he finished his working life cleaning the players' boots at West Ham United.

Two Plymouth Argyle fans, Greg Foxsmith and Matt Tiller, launched the Jack Leslie Campaign in 2020 to celebrate the player's achievements. They raised £140,000 towards a statue of Leslie at Plymouth's Home Park.

THE BALLAD OF JACK LESLIE

66 *A wizard in defence or attack, Called up for England but they sent him back, 'Cos they'd not seen a picture of young Jack, And he never got to play because he was black.* 99

by **Matt Tiller**

Jack Leslie worked as boot boy for West Ham United during the 1960s and 1970s.

Football's Windrush Story

Hundreds of new arrivals from British colonies in the Caribbean – immaculately dressed and clutching a few belongings – stepped off the *Empire Windrush* passenger ship in London in 1948. Being British citizens, they were invited to rebuild Britain after the Second World War. The country was broke and desperately short of workers.

In the years that followed, the trickle of people who arrived at Tilbury Docks became a steady stream as tens of thousands of Commonwealth British subjects answered the call to help the "mother country".

The Windrush Generation, as the new arrivals became known, worked in the new National Health Service, transport and other industries across the country. They helped revive an economy that had been left decimated after seven years of war.

Before long, some of the big cities came alive with new music such as Calypso, exotic food, innovative art and new writing. Their presence transformed Britain's cultural landscape. Eventually, the children of the Windrush Generation made their mark in English football.

AWESOME OFFSPRING

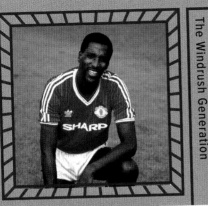

Viv Anderson
Playing career 1974–95

FOOTBALL'S CHAMPIONS OF CHANGE

Viv Anderson was the first black footballer officially to play for the England team. Part of the Windrush Generation, his dad, Audley, sailed from Jamaica to Nottingham on the SS *Auriga* in 1954, where his wife, Myrtle, joined him a year later. They often felt unwelcome, which was typical for many from the Windrush Generation.

Anderson won the first of 30 England caps against Czechoslovakia in 1978, and enjoyed an outstanding career at Nottingham Forest, Arsenal and Manchester United.

Hope Powell
Playing career 1978–98

FOOTBALL'S CHAMPIONS OF CHANGE

Born to Jamaican parents, Hope Powell grew up in south London. She served as an inspirational midfielder for Millwall, Fulham, Bromley and Croydon, and scored 35 goals for England.

In 1998, she became the first black England coach to lead the Lionesses.

After landing the job, she grew her dreadlocks as a statement of pride in who she is. She took the team to the final of Women's Euro 2009 and remained in charge for 15 years.

Powell is now the manager of Brighton in the Women's Super League.

HATE POLITICS

The lives of the Windrush Generation were made even more difficult after an infamous speech by the Conservative MP Enoch Powell in 1968. Powell strongly disagreed with mass immigration and used racial insults in what became known as the *"Rivers of Blood"* speech.

The speech in Birmingham predicted a war between races if immigration did not stop. He claimed that "in this country in 15 or 20 years' time the black man will have the whip hand over the white man." He suggested paying immigrants to leave.

Powell's words caused outrage. Disturbingly, many people supported him too. His predictions never came true, but the speech led to an increase in violent attacks on people from ethnic minorities and left many communities living in fear.

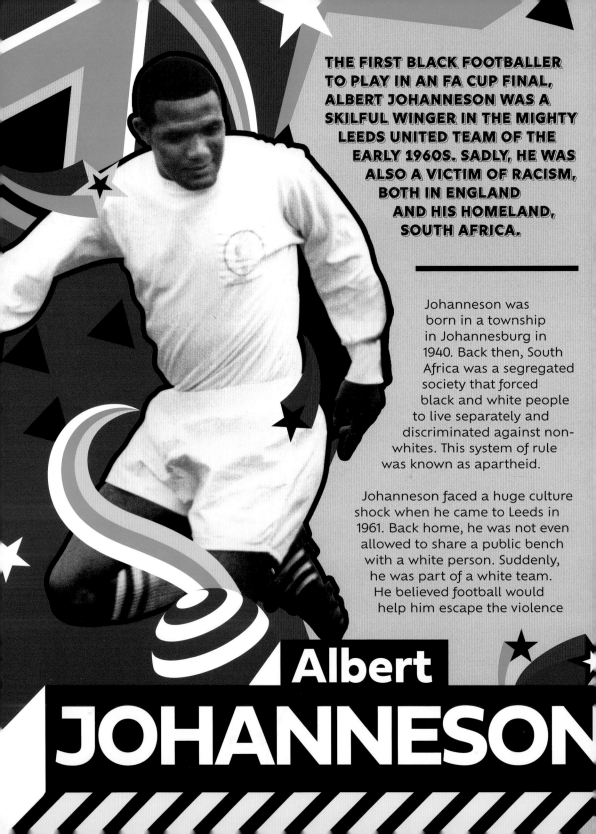

THE FIRST BLACK FOOTBALLER TO PLAY IN AN FA CUP FINAL, ALBERT JOHANNESON WAS A SKILFUL WINGER IN THE MIGHTY LEEDS UNITED TEAM OF THE EARLY 1960S. SADLY, HE WAS ALSO A VICTIM OF RACISM, BOTH IN ENGLAND AND HIS HOMELAND, SOUTH AFRICA.

Johanneson was born in a township in Johannesburg in 1940. Back then, South Africa was a segregated society that forced black and white people to live separately and discriminated against non-whites. This system of rule was known as apartheid.

Johanneson faced a huge culture shock when he came to Leeds in 1961. Back home, he was not even allowed to share a public bench with a white person. Suddenly, he was part of a white team. He believed football would help him escape the violence

Albert
JOHANNESON

and racism of his youth, but it was still there under the surface. Although Johanneson was loved by the Leeds fans, he suffered endless hostility at away grounds. His dazzling skills helped the team win promotion to the first division and reach the 1965 cup final.

Before kick-off, Johanneson suffered vicious abuse. Some blamed him for his team's poor display in the final, which they lost 2–1 to Liverpool. He did not perform well at Wembley but neither did his team – and yet he was singled out.

> 66 All I could hear was a cacophony of Zulu-like noises coming from the terraces. It was dreadful. I could barely hear myself think for those screams. I wanted to run back down the tunnel. 99
>
> Johanneson reflecting on 1965 Cup final

He never recovered from the abuse. He left Leeds in 1970 before retiring two years later. Tragically, he turned to alcohol to numb the sadness of his life and died alone in his flat in 1995.

The footballer's gravestone is inscribed with lines from the poem 'Still I Rise' by the American writer and civil rights activist Maya Angelou. His career and the struggles of many other black players of the era coincided with the height of the civil rights movement, which campaigned to abolish racial segregation and discrimination in the USA.

AND STILL I RISE

Out of the huts
of history's shame
I rise
Up from a past
that's rooted in pain
I rise
I'm a black ocean,
leaping and wide,
Welling and swelling
I bear the tide.

Maya Angelou's words inscribed on Johanneson's gravestone

ALBERT LOUIS JOHANNESON

Born and raised in South Africa, he found a new life in England. A mesmerising left winger, he made 200 appearances for Leeds United from 1961 to 1969 scoring 67 goals, playing an integral role in helping the club win promotion to the First Division in 1964.

In 1965, he became the first black African to play in an F.A. Cup Final.

1940–1995

A blue plaque was unveiled in Leeds in 2019 to mark Johanneson's contribution to Leeds United.

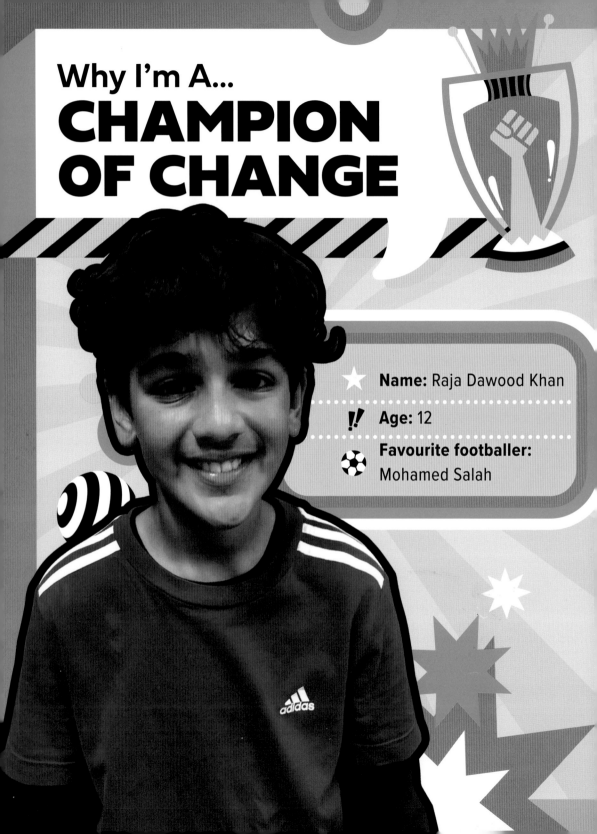

Why I'm A...
CHAMPION
OF CHANGE

Name: Raja Dawood Khan

Age: 12

Favourite footballer:
Mohamed Salah

My dad was born and raised in Pakistan. My mum was born in Britain, but both of her parents are Pakistani, so I suppose I see myself as a British Asian.

I first became interested in football when I saw Messi play for Barcelona against Real Madrid on TV. I really liked the way he played, so I asked my dad to take me to play football. After I scored my first goal, I was hooked. I really liked how it made me feel and that's how it all started. I am a midfielder.

There aren't many professional south Asian footballers in Britain, so I am hoping to be one of the few that makes it. Asked which country I would choose to play for if I am good enough – England or Pakistan – I'd choose England. Football isn't really part of Pakistan's culture, anyway. Normally, cricket is more popular there. My dad plays cricket too, but I prefer football. When I saw Messi I just fell in love with the game. I am also a big fan of Mohamed Salah.

I have had a few problems with racism in the game. One time, during a match, I challenged for the ball a bit too hard, but said sorry to the kid right away. He called me a *"curry muncher"* because of my colour. I started crying because I was upset. I told my mum, but I didn't want to start a big argument. The kid got banned for two weeks. He didn't say anything offensive after that. The punishment did teach him a lesson that

> **He called me a 'curry muncher' because of my colour.**

you shouldn't be calling other people racist names. We made up and became friends again so it was all right. That was when I was seven. People still call me racist names sometimes, but nowadays I stand up to it right away.

> **There aren't many professional Asian footballers in Britain...**

> **...so I am hoping to be one of the few that makes it.**

4

THE UGLY SIDE OF THE BEAUTIFUL GAME

Thanks to the brilliance of players such as Pelé and Jairzinho, Brazil won the 1970 World Cup playing 'the beautiful game'. The first international sporting tournament beamed into people's homes in colour, it had a huge global impact that inspired the next generation of black footballers.

In the same period, some largely white working-class men in England were disillusioned with their place in the world, primarily because of the increasing lack of jobs and opportunities. They showed their frustration through football hooliganism and sometimes directed their hatred at black players. In response, some inspirational figures took a stand.

Dawn Of A New Era

In their bright yellow shirts and playing the kind of dazzling football never witnessed before, a multiracial team representing Brazil won the 1970 FIFA World Cup in style. The beautiful game was on display in all its glory in Mexico – delighting and mesmerising millions of people watching around the globe.

It was the first FIFA World Cup broadcast on television in colour and made superstars of Brazil's contingent of black players, such as Jairzinho, Carlos Alberto and Marco Antônio, led by one of football's greatest ever icons, Pelé.

Perhaps for the first time, a group of black and mixed heritage people was seen on the world stage, looking cool, confident and in complete control of the artistry on show. This challenged the stereotypically negative portrayal of black people in the media generally. Kenneth Wolstenholme, the famous British TV commentator, was almost lost for words when he described one of Pelé's most iconic plays – an amazingly skilful dummy – to deceive an opposition goalkeeper in Brazil's semi-final match against Uruguay: *"Oh, what... what genius!"* was all he could say watching Pelé in that moment.

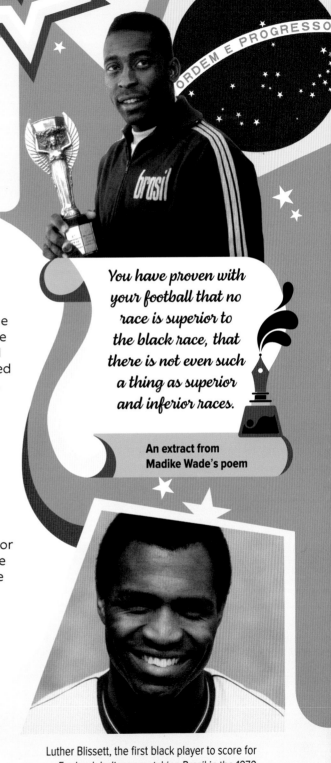

Pelé's legacy

There were famous black sport stars before Pelé, of course, but Pelé was the first global black sporting celebrity. He is the only footballer to win the World Cup three times and was often described in Brazil as *O Rei*, meaning 'The King'. Pelé's success had special meaning particularly in Africa. The day after Brazil's 1970 World Cup triumph, the French journal *Africasia* published a poem penned by Madike Wade, one of its Senegal correspondents, which honoured Pelé.

For decades, black footballers were portrayed as lazy, lacking intelligence or the ability to take responsibility on the pitch. Pelé's brilliance made nonsense of these notions. Although Pelé never took a vocal stance against racism, his achievements and professionalism spoke volumes and helped dispel the false image of black athletes.

You have proven with your football that no race is superior to the black race, that there is not even such a thing as superior and inferior races.

An extract from Madike Wade's poem

Luther Blissett, the first black player to score for England, believes watching Brazil in the 1970 World Cup inspired him to become a footballer.

55

Reality Check

Brazil's glory in the thrilling summer of 1970 promised a brighter future for football. But the state of the game in England at the start of the new decade couldn't have been more different, where Britain's minority ethnic communities were in the firing line.

The first cases of what is now known as football hooliganism – violent and disorderly behaviour by fans – were recorded as far back as the end of the 19th century. Rival football fans have been involved in violent clashes with each other from time to time ever since.

In the 1960s and 70s, this frightening phenomenon took on an even more sinister turn as troublemakers began targeting black and minority ethnic supporters and players. Racist abuse from the terraces towards players

and violence against black and Asian supporters became common. Far-right political organisations, such as the National Front, began recruiting among football supporters, blaming non-white immigrants for the country's social and economic problems.

A minority of fans were attracted by their message and felt empowered to be part of the political group. The football stands gave them a regular platform to voice their racial hatred and indulge in violence.

Targeting players

Non-white players were subjected to terrible abuse. For most, it was an isolating and sometimes frightening experience. Leyton Orient players **Bobby Fisher** and **Laurie Cunningham** narrowly avoided being hit by a kitchen knife thrown by a group of Millwall followers at their home ground, The Den, in 1974.

The player **Dave Busby**'s experience at Barrow illustrates the kind of suspicion black people felt they were under in the 1970s. In order to defend himself against some of the lazy stereotypes that existed, he felt the need to reassure his local newsagent when he first entered the shop that he was there to buy a newspaper and not commit a robbery.

WHAT IS STEREOTYPING?

We all tend to group people into different categories. It helps us to make sense of a world filled with so much difference, but this can also create an unfair and inaccurate picture of those other people. This is stereotyping.

Ethnic minority footballers are often the victims of racial stereotyping and made to feel inferior. For example, black players are regularly portrayed as fast and strong but not thinkers of the game, and as players who can't be trusted in positions of authority, such as captaincy on the pitch. The truth is that everyone, whatever their background, is unique.

TACTLESS TV

In the 1970s British TV sitcom, *Love Thy Neighbour*, a West Indian husband and wife move next door to a white couple. The white man immediately feels uncomfortable, suggesting that there is something to fear from their black neighbours. The comedy relied on deeply offensive stereotypes to get laughs, presenting the West Indian couple as racially and culturally inferior to their white neighbours.

IN 1968, 16-YEAR-OLD STRIKER CLYDE BEST ARRIVED FROM BERMUDA FOR A TRIAL AT WEST HAM UNITED. AN ATHLETIC CENTRE FORWARD, HE SOON SECURED HIS PLACE IN THE TEAM, PLAYING IN THE FIRST DIVISION ALONGSIDE THREE ENGLAND WORLD-CUP WINNERS, BOBBY MOORE, GEOFF HURST AND MARTIN PETERS.

The dream move for Best was a nightmare in other respects. He often faced monkey chants and abusive language from the stands, and even threats at times. On one occasion, he received a letter in the post warning him that acid would be thrown in his face the next time he stepped onto the pitch.

The letter was reported to the police, who provided a protective barrier as the players ran out of the tunnel. The match ended without incident, but the threat shows the level of hostility faced by black players in the 1970s.

Clyde
BEST

> **"** *The best way to react to stuff like that is to stick the ball in the net and you shut everybody's mouth.* **"**
>
> Clyde Best

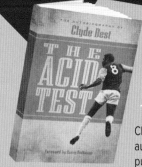

Clyde Best's searing autobiography was published in 2016.

Best suffered horrific racist abuse during his eight years at West Ham but he never retaliated. He believed scoring goals and winning was the perfect response to his tormentors. Years later, he made a mischievous dig at the writer of that sinister letter by calling his autobiography *The Acid Test*.

Best even faced hostility from some West Ham supporters. Sometimes he was unfairly blamed when the team lost or performed poorly. But that only had the effect of making him try even harder and he went on to score 58 goals in more than 200 appearances for the club.

Best was often supported by his team-mates and his manager Ron Greenwood, who had given him his first opportunity to play. In 1972, the same West Ham manager fielded three black players when Best lined up alongside Ade Coker and Clive Charles. It was the first time this had ever happened in England.

Best went on to play abroad and manage a national team for Bermuda. A giant figure in West Ham's history, he remains a frequent visitor. As the first black football star of the colour TV era in England, he became a figurehead to the generation of players that followed.

West Ham United team picture taken in 1972 with Clyde Best circled.

Making A Stand

Confronted by racism from the terraces, black footballers in the 1970s mostly stayed silent. Instead of fighting back, many channelled their feelings into delivering better performances, mainly because they believed no one would support them if they spoke out.

Unlike now, there was little debate about the subject in the media. Booing and monkey noises aimed at players were ignored in football commentaries. Broadcasters at the time believed it was wrong to give any airtime to the racist behaviour of ignorant spectators.

One commentator, Gerald Sinstadt, was the first to break with protocol during a match between Manchester United and West Bromwich Albion in 1978. West Brom's three black players were barracked relentlessly during the game at Old Trafford. Sinstadt called the behaviour "unsavoury" and lacking in sportsmanship. The fact that he didn't condemn the incident more forcefully, though reveals the attitudes of the time.

Despite this culture of silence, however, there were a few players who dared to make a stand. Leyton Orient's Bobby Fisher and Laurie Cunningham were spat on by followers of Millwall in the match at The Den in 1974 (see page 57). At the final whistle, in an act of defiance, both players made a Black Power Salute towards the home fans.

WHAT IS THE BLACK POWER SALUTE?

At the 1968 Olympic Games in Mexico, USA athletes **Tommie Smith** and **John Carlos** – who won gold and bronze medals in the men's 200 metres – each raised a black-gloved fist on the podium. It was a gesture intended to show solidarity with oppressed black people worldwide. At the time, black men and women in the USA were being attacked and denied their rights because of the colour of their skin.

The pair were expelled from the Games, but their actions became a powerful symbol that inspired future generations of sportsmen and women fighting for equality.

BERRY HITS OUT!

With his distinctive hairstyle and combative manner on the pitch, **George Berry** was a cult figure whose career spanned from the 1970s to the early 90s. On one occasion, Berry was racially abused as he left the pitch. The Wolves centre half went into the crowd and tussled with the spectator who made the jibe. The incident received little publicity and neither man was charged by the police. Berry now admits that he's not proud of his actions that day, but believes he had to stand up for his principles.

The Three Degrees

A black American all-female vocal group called the Three Degrees scored a string of hit records in the 1970s. They enjoyed success in England too and inspired the affectionate nickname given to three brilliant, pioneering black footballers – **Cyrille Regis**, **Laurie Cunningham** and **Brendon Batson**.

In the 1970s, it was still rare to see black players in English professional football. By 1978, West Bromwich Albion became the first club to regularly feature three black players in their team. It had a significant impact.

Regis was a deadly striker who terrorised defenders. Cunningham dazzled with his skilful play on the wing, and Batson was a stylish attacking full-back. Together, they helped make West Brom one of the most watchable teams in the country and attracted a new generation of black British football fans.

The West Brom team of 1978–79 finished second in the title race, but they would no doubt have been popular champions had they managed to beat the all-conquering Liverpool side of that era.

(L-R) Cunningham, Batson and Regis with the singing group sensation The Three Degrees in 1979.

Trio under fire

Sadly, all three players had to endure racist abuse and intimidation during matches and in their everyday lives. It often went beyond the monkey chanting and banana-throwing that was already commonplace in the English game.

When Cyrille Regis was called up to the England squad, he received a bullet through the post, accompanied by a letter which read: "If you put a foot on our Wembley turf you'll get one of these through your knees."

Laurie Cunningham had a petrol bomb thrown through his front door. He was confronted with familiar stereotypes about black footballers being ill-disciplined, lazy or lacking mental strength. He rose above it all by going on to become the first Englishman to play for the Spanish giants Real Madrid.

Brendon Batson has spoken of the disgusting treatment the trio suffered, particularly on trips away from home.

The brilliance of Regis, Cunningham and Batson helped silence some of the racist voices and West Brom were undoubtedly the uncrowned people's champions of the 78–79 season.

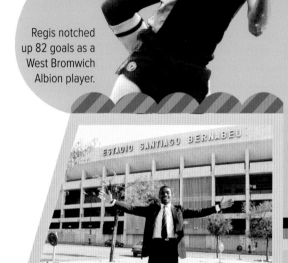

Regis notched up 82 goals as a West Bromwich Albion player.

Cunningham outside Real Madrid's Santiago Bernabéu Stadium on 26 October 1982.

66 *We'd get off the coach at away matches and the National Front would be right there in your face… We'd get to the players' entrance and there'd be spit on my jacket or Cyrille's shirt.* 99

Brendon Batson

Hooliganism Takes Hold

Sadly, hooliganism and racism were a part of the English football landscape in the 1970s and 1980s. The people involved were often young, jobless and disenchanted white working-class men. They needed to feel part of something. Joining a violent group alongside others with the same frustrations satisfied that need. Minorities and rival supporters gave them a focus to channel their feelings.

Paul Canoville was the first black player to represent Chelsea. When he warmed up before his debut against Crystal Palace in 1982, he was racially abused by his own Chelsea supporters. He even experienced slurs and prejudice from a few team-mates and claimed that racism wasn't taken seriously by his own club.

John Barnes scored one of England's greatest goals in a 2–0 victory over Brazil in 1984. Racist England followers who supported the National Front taunted him on the flight home. They claimed England only won 1–0, rejecting Barnes' goal because he was black.

"Dazzler socks racists"

SKY BLUES

AGAINST THE NAZIS

"The new Nazis of soccer, who have adopted the nauseating practice of jeering at coloured players to try to put them off their game, got the order of the boot in a big way at Coventry.

Outside the ground an action group of City fans distributed thousands of leaflets urging that Highfield Road should become a no-go area for those racists who abuse coloured players"

After the Ipswich match, the Mirror printed this report by Frank Taylor. Meanwhile, the Coventry Telegraph responded with a deafening silence.

Anti Nazi League

Anti Nazi League

DAZZLER SOCKS THE RACISTS

In 1978, Coventry City's mascot, Dazzler, led an effort to stop racist abuse in the crowd. Dazzler handed out leaflets outside the stadium, opposing the National Front and urged fans to help keep racism out of their ground. It helped pave the way for growing anti-racist campaigns later on.

HORROR AT HEYSEL

English clubs were banned from European competitions for five years after the Heysel Stadium disaster in Brussels in 1985. Violent clashes between Liverpool and Juventus fans during the European Cup final led to 39 deaths of mainly Italian fans. It became known as European football's darkest hour. Hooliganism was often seen as the 'English disease', even though violence and racism were widespread in other countries too.

The tragedy at Heysel forced the authorities to take action. New laws were passed that tackled hooliganism and the racist element that was often present. It became an offence to take part in racist chanting at matches, and those found guilty faced bans from grounds, fines and prison sentences.

In remembrance of the 39 supporters who lost their lives at the Heysel Stadium

May 29th 1985

IN MEMORIA E AMICIZIA

A wreath at the memorial and friendship plaque at Liverpool's Anfield Stadium.

Why I'm A...
CHAMPION OF CHANGE

Name: Lauren Thomas

Age: 10

Favourite footballers:
Ella Toone and
Alessia Russo

I am Lauren from Sheffield. My dad is black and my mum white. I play as a striker for Charnock Ridgeway girls' football team. I can only remember experiencing racism in football once.

At the end of a game, we were shaking hands with the players of the other team. One girl whispered something about me to her friend and then when I went to shake her hand, she ignored me. I was a bit upset but tried not to think about it.

I remember when Marcus Rashford and those other black players missed penalties for England at UEFA Euro 2020, and were abused. Everyone misses the goal sometimes. But it's difficult for any player to deal with abuse from their own fans. Those fans behaved so badly that they risked losing a valuable player from their team. If it happened to me, I reckon I would have tried to do something to stop them or even leave the team. I am surprised they stayed. They were very brave.

It was my dad who got me into football. I went to a football camp for a few weeks. The camp had a mix of boys and girls, but when we played the boys just hogged the ball and only passed it to each other. I think they thought the girls wouldn't be as good as them. Because of their attitude, I started playing girls' football instead and have made progress. I love it.

> **One girl whispered something about me to her friend...**

> **...and then when I went to shake her hand, she ignored me.**

I went to three matches at Bramall Lane during Women's Euros 2022, including the semi-final match between the Lionesses and Sweden. They were great games. My favourite players are Ella Toone and Alessia Russo. They have all the skills and score lots of goals. It's brilliant to see. I do a lot of sport and try to play as much as I can. I suppose I am a little bit of a trailblazer as well.

> **I do a lot of sport... I suppose I am a little bit of a trailblazer as well.**

5

THE WINDS OF CHANGE

In the summer of 1990, England enjoyed its best World Cup in years. Featuring some outstanding black players, the team won the hearts of the nation and spawned a new generation of football fans across the country. The tournament proved a turning point as supporters demanded a greater say in the game's future and called for action in combating the ugly stain of racism.

Here was an opportunity for English football to modernise, particularly after the formation of the Premier League in 1992. Seizing the moment, campaigners faced some opposition, but they also found strong support from players and fans. As England made strides in the fight against prejudice, other parts of the world began to follow.

The New Nineties

People still talk about the 1990 World Cup held in Italy. They remember the dramatic BBC theme tune Nessun Dorma, which was sung by the great Italian opera singer Luciano Pavarotti. And how could they forget England's glorious run to the semi-finals or its heart-breaking defeat to West Germany on penalties?

Most of all, people remember 'Gazza's tears', when England's Paul 'Gazza' Gascoigne couldn't contain his emotion after receiving a yellow card. In that dramatic moment, the star midfielder realised he would be suspended from playing in the final if England went through to that match.

But the tournament was important for another reason. Before 1990, no black player had ever started for England in a major competition. Bobby Robson's World Cup squad, however, included three black stars. Each had an influential role to play in a team that looked like worldbeaters.

This new-look England side arrived at the World Cup at a time when the game at home was in a bad way. Following the 1985 Heysel Stadium disaster (see page 65), English teams were banned from European club competitions, while the threat of racism and hooliganism was discouraging fans from attending home matches. The mood was summed up by a newspaper article in *The Sunday Times*, which described English football as "a slum sport, played in slum stadiums and increasingly watched by slum people".

THE THREE AMIGOS

"God Save Our Gracious Queen, Long live..."

JOHN BARNES

GAZZA

DES WALKER

PAUL PARKER

John Barnes, Paul Parker and Des Walker were the three history-making black players in England's squad for the 1990 World Cup. They were all in top form when the tournament started.

Among the best players in the world, Liverpool's Barnes would become one of the jewels in England's crown. Walker, a lightning-fast defender for Nottingham Forest, was so good that fans sang, *"You'll never beat Des Walker"*. Meanwhile, QPR's Parker proved himself to be a highly adaptable defender who could play full back or in the centre of defence.

Game changer

England's run to the Semis at the World Cup marked the dawn of a new era. Keen to attract the world's best footballers and more international fans, English clubs and TV companies began discussing the creation of a brand new league. In 1992, the Premier League was launched.

Times were changing as supporters from diverse backgrounds now demanded to be heard. In fact, the 1990s heralded a golden opportunity to tackle the persistent problem of racism on the terraces.

The Law Takes Aim

The 1990s may have been the start of a new age for the English game, but there were still many obstacles to overcome when it came to defeating racism. For a start, the Football Association was run exclusively by white men and very few of them seemed engaged with the issue. In contrast, ethnic minority players understood the problem only too well. Many even avoided taking family and friends to matches to shield them from racial abuse.

The country's first priority was to try to make football grounds less hostile to ethnic minority players and supporters. In 1991, the government took a major step by passing a new law, known as the Football Offences Act. Under this new act, the police were given extra powers to stamp out racist chanting along with other antisocial behaviour, at football grounds.

Meanwhile, former black players initiated campaign groups, such as Kick It Out and Show Racism the Red Card (see page 78), that worked closely with football clubs, encouraging them to

Football (Offences)
Act 1991

LONDON

identify offenders in their stadiums and ban them from returning. For decades, players and supporters from ethnic minorities had been powerless to prevent abuse. While some in football had merely turned a blind eye to the problem, others felt it was wrong to draw attention to an offensive minority. Now, in the decade when England embraced three black players at the World Cup, the new attitude was to confront the issue head on.

JUSTIN FASHANU (1961–98)

At the start of a decade that saw so much progress for ethnic minority footballers, Justin Fashanu hit the headlines in 1990 when he became the first top-level player to come out as gay. But Fashanu, who had already endured racism from the terraces, now faced double discrimination – as a man who was both black and gay. Offered little support from his club or his family, Fashanu tragically took his own life at the age of 37.

Daily NEWS 40p

£1m SOCCER STAR: I AM GAY

Justin Fashanu Confesses

Justin Fashanu featured in the England U-21 side 11 times between 1980 and 1982, scoring five goals.

IAN WRIGHT GOT HIS BREAK LATE IN FOOTBALL. AS A TEENAGER, HE HAD TRIALS WITH SEVERAL CLUBS BUT FAILED TO SECURE A CONTRACT. INSTEAD, HE WORKED AS A PLASTERER WHILE PLAYING NON-LEAGUE FOOTBALL. ON THE VERGE OF GIVING UP HIS DREAM, HE WAS SIGNED BY CRYSTAL PALACE AT THE AGE OF 21 – AND THE REST IS HISTORY...

Born in south London to Jamaican parents, Wright was the third of three brothers. Abandoned by their father when they were very young, the kids were raised by their mum, Nesta, and cruel stepfather, who often dealt out violent abuse to the family.

Wright managed to overcome his traumatic start in life, but he still carries the emotional scars of his childhood. He revelled in his image as a 'ragamuffin' or 'roadman' – the Jamaican slang for someone who is tough and streetwise.

Ian WRIGHT

After a short spell in prison, Wright became determined to make it as a professional footballer and, in 1985, his efforts earned him a contract at Crystal Palace, where he spent six years alongside fellow striker Mark Bright in a successful double act – Wright and Bright. The club won promotion to the first division in 1989, and Wright was later voted Palace's player of the century.

Wright moved to Arsenal in 1991 for a club-record transfer fee of £2.5 million. Having scored a hat trick on his league debut, the striker went on to score 185 goals in 288 appearances. He won the Premier League, the FA Cup and the League Cup, and earned 33 caps for England before ending his career after stints at West Ham, Nottingham Forest, Celtic and Burnley.

Since retiring from playing, 'Wrighty', as he is affectionately known, has become a well-known pundit on the BBC's Match Of The Day. A passionate supporter of women's football, he has demanded more opportunities for girls and women to play.

An outspoken critic of racism in football, Wright has spoken about the abuse he received from the terraces and online.

> 66 *You feel dehumanised. You feel like nothing. There's nothing you can do. You are helpless.* 99
>
> Ian Wright speaking about the abuse he's received during his playing career

He has called for greater education for those brought in front of the courts charged with sending grossly offensive messages on social media.

Staying true to his south London roots, Wright has become an inspiring role model to youngsters from similar disadvantaged backgrounds. In 2000, he was awarded the MBE for services to football.

Ian Wright received his MBE from Queen Elizabeth shortly after retiring from professional football.

> 66 *This is the proudest I have ever felt about any England side.* 99
>
> Ian Wright talking after England's Lionesses won Euro 2022

Campaigns For Change

The positive strides made in tackling racism in football in the 1990s were due in large part to organised campaigns for change. For the first time, people came together in large numbers determined to make a difference.

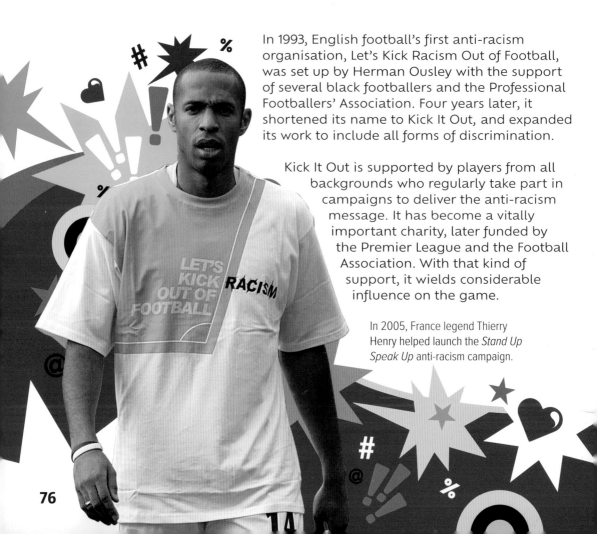

In 1993, English football's first anti-racism organisation, Let's Kick Racism Out of Football, was set up by Herman Ousley with the support of several black footballers and the Professional Footballers' Association. Four years later, it shortened its name to Kick It Out, and expanded its work to include all forms of discrimination.

Kick It Out is supported by players from all backgrounds who regularly take part in campaigns to deliver the anti-racism message. It has become a vitally important charity, later funded by the Premier League and the Football Association. With that kind of support, it wields considerable influence on the game.

In 2005, France legend Thierry Henry helped launch the *Stand Up Speak Up* anti-racism campaign.

On a mission

Sadly, racist abuse can take place in many different situations – in a football crowd, during a school match or online. Now, any football fan can report such incidents using Kick It Out's website or phone app and be confident that it will be dealt with.

The charity teaches young players in Premier League academies, as well as their parents and coaches, about racism and discrimination. Its overarching message is that if football is to be played and enjoyed equally by everyone – whatever the colour of their skin – it is up to all of us to stand up to any form of racism. The organisation even speaks face to face with fans who have abused others to help stop such incidents from happening again.

> 66 We all know Kick It Out shouldn't have to exist... But right now we're here to put an end to every form of discrimination. We won't stop until it stops. 99
>
> Kick It Out's mission statement

LORD HERMAN OUSLEY

Part of the Windrush Generation (see page 46), Herman Ousley arrived in Britain from Guyana in the Caribbean at the age of 11. His experiences of encountering racism as a young football fan in south London spurred him into setting up Kick It Out, in 1993. Although he and his co-founders faced a brick wall of opposition from some people inside the game who were worried it would damage their reputation, the men refused to give up.

As well as leading the charity for 26 years, Ousley has had an impressive career in local government and has been at the forefront of fighting racism in many different organisations.

Player Turns Activist

In 1995, Trinidad and Tobago goalkeeper **Shaka Hislop** had recently joined Newcastle United. Filling up his car up with petrol one day, he was confronted by a group of youths hurling racist abuse at him. However, their attitude changed when one of them recognised Hislop and asked for his autograph instead.

The incident proved to be a light-bulb moment for Hislop, who realised he could use his position as a famous footballer to challenge racist attitudes. In 1996, he helped establish Show Racism the Red Card, which promotes famous footballers as anti-racism role models and combats prejudice through anti-racism education.

Today, thousands of young people attend the charity's classes, which challenge stereotypes and negative attitudes in society. The charity also makes educational films with star players, such as Liverpool's **Trent Alexander-Arnold** and **Demi Stokes** from the England Lionesses, who won the UEFA Women's Euro 2022.

Football unites

In the 1990s, an alarming increase in racial harassment near Sheffield United's ground motivated a group of fans to do something about it. Founded in 1995, Football Unites, Racism Divides (FURD) has become a leading light in the battle against discrimination.

FURD staff go into schools to teach young people about the importance of fighting racism. The charity also provides coaching courses for youngsters, using football to break down barriers and promote better understanding between communities.

The talent of Manchester City and England defender **Kyle Walker** was first spotted at one of FURD's coaching courses. He was recommended to Sheffield United, where he began his journey as a professional footballer.

Kyle Walker as a young boy at FURD in 1995 (above) and as an England player in 2020.

> 66 *Just be yourself, it doesn't matter if you are Asian or black or white. We are all the same. We all have a heart. We all have blood in our veins and that's it.* 99
>
> Kyle Walker, Manchester City and England

BRENDON BATSON

An elegant full back for West Bromwich Albion and a member of the so-called 'Three Degrees' (see page 62), Brendon Batson has also enjoyed a second career as a respected football administrator. Motivated by his experiences as a player, he has become an influential figure in the campaign to target racism. Batson served as the deputy chief executive of the players' union, the Professional Footballers' Association. In 2015, he was awarded an OBE for services to football.

Protests From The Pitch

When a footballer reacts to an incident of racial abuse from an opponent or the crowd, it is a often a response provoked by anger, pain, humiliation and disgust – and it reflects the deeply wounding nature of racism.

In the past, many players who experienced racism suffered in silence. Nowadays, because of changing attitudes, players feel more confident about seeking justice for themselves both on and off the pitch.

The examples on the next page show how player reactions, in the heat of the moment, helped to highlight the issue and bring about change:

OWNING IT...

GOING BANANAS

In 2014, Barcelona defender **Dani Alves** picked up and ate a banana thrown at him during a *La Liga* match against Villareal. The action inspired a clever social media campaign in which famous players from around the world shared pictures of themselves eating a banana with the hashtag #weareallmonkeys.

ON BENDED KNEE

Following the 2020 murder of George Floyd (a black American killed by a white policeman), France striker **Marcus Thuram** was the first footballer to take the knee after scoring in the Bundesliga. The gesture was first made by American football player Colin Kaepernick in 2016, in protest against racism in the USA.

WALKING THE WALK

In 2022, Bolton Wanderers players walked off the pitch to protest about alleged racist abuse from the crowd at Morecambe. Bolton Wanderers manager **Ian Evatt** fiercely defended the stand his side took: "If one of us gets abused, we all get abused and we all stick together."

SINGING A DIFFERENT SONG

In a bid to tackle hate instead of spreading it, young people in Middlesbrough created a new chant for fans to sing. It was part of an arts and music project organised by the club's own charitable foundation. The MFC Foundation reaches out to football-mad youngsters who already have a passion for the game. The organisation uses football to inspire youngsters so that they have a better chance to improve their quality of life.

The children worked with young rapper Shakk to produce their chant to the tune of the famous S Club 7 song 'Reach'. They made a video at Middlesbrough's Riverside Stadium, which was named after the club's home ground.

Europe Takes A Stand

Today, opportunities for ethnic minority footballers to play the game professionally exist right across Europe. More than 500 African footballers bring excitement and variety to European leagues. Portugal attracts Brazilians because of a shared history, while France has plenty of home-grown ethnic minority players whose parents and grandparents arrived from former colonies.

However, discrimination in some parts of the continent, especially in Eastern Europe and Italy, still exists. For example, extremists who follow Russian club Zenit St Petersburg stated on their website that black players were not welcome. In Poland, Nazi symbols have been seen in football crowds and some rival fans casually use the word 'Jew' as a term of abuse towards each other.

Senegalese star Sadio Mané lifts the trophy after Liverpool beat Tottenham in the 2019 UEFA Champions League final.

Discrimination detectives

In 1999, Football Against Racism in Europe was formed to challenge discrimination, particularly in the east. The organisation sends undercover observers to matches to look out for racist incidents and report them to the authorities.

But, of course, the problem extends far beyond Eastern Europe. Sicily-born striker **Mario Balotelli** was frequently a target for followers of the Italian national team because of his Ghanaian heritage. *Non ci sono negri Italiani* (There are no Italian blacks) was a racist chant directed at Balotelli by Juventus supporters. Efforts to confront racism in Italian football have sometimes been clumsy, such as when the top league, *Serie A*, used paintings of monkeys as part of a 2019 anti-discrimination campaign.

In Germany, ethnic minority players, such as **Mesut Ozil** – the son of Turkish immigrants – have been criticised for not singing the national anthem before Germany's matches and unfairly blamed when the team loses. Now, *Fanprojekte* (Fan Projects) helps to educate young fans, while clubs such as Bayern Munich run initiatives to support refugees.

WALKING THE LINE

In 2013, racist chanting directed at German-Ghanaian midfielder **Kevin-Prince Boateng**, during a friendly between Italian sides AC Milan and Pro Patria, caused the player to remove his shirt and leave the pitch. His AC Milan teammates followed, and the match ended abruptly.

The player's bold move attracted worldwide attention and changed the way football handles the issue. Now, if racist abuse occurs, the referee has the power to suspend the match and send the players to the changing rooms. The police are informed, and the match can even be abandoned. Boateng became the first global ambassador of an anti-discrimination taskforce set up by FIFA.

The Global Fight Against Racism

Three decades on from the launch of Kick It Out in England, there are efforts to tackle racism in football around the world. Campaigns have spread to every continent, but in some parts of the world they still face opposition.

ROMANIA

Launched in **2007**, Racism Breaks the Game led to a change in the way the media reports racist incidents in football in Eastern Europe. Roma minorities have often been the target of abuse, but the group started a movement to combat the problem.

SOUTH AMERICA

In **2013**, players from Brazilian club Gremio used the club's colours, blue, black and white, as the title for a campaign against racism. Football in South America has a long history of discrimination against players of African descent, though the subject has only rarely been discussed.

AUSTRALIA

Football Federation Australia and Professional Footballers Australia launched a joint initiative, Erase Racism, in **2014**. The country is commonly seen as multicultural, but Adelaide City's Kusini Yengi was sent gorilla emojis after his team beat Melbourne Victory in **2021**.

RUSSIA

CSKA Moscow fan Robert Ustian launched a grassroots anti-racism campaign in Russia – the only one of its kind in the country – before the **2018** World Cup. Swastikas have appeared at games in Russia and there was violence by Russian neo-Nazis at Euro **2016** in France.

JAPAN

Sports brand Nike began an advertising campaign in **2020** featuring three young footballers facing racism in Japan. It has been an issue in the J-League for a few years. Some praised it, while others said it unfairly represented Japan and called for a boycott of Nike products.

USA

In **2020**, Major League Soccer in America launched a campaign to combat racism and increase opportunities for people from minority ethnic backgrounds to get involved in the game. The MLS clubs pledged $1 million to fund the initiative.

INDIA

Since his anti-prejudice plea on social media in **2018**, footballer Sunil Chhetri has become a figurehead in the fight against racism in Indian football and wider society. The country is divided along lines of caste, and darker-skinned people often face discrimination.

THE LEGENDARY FORMER FRANCE CAPTAIN ZINEDINE ZIDANE IS REGARDED AS ONE OF THE GREATEST FOOTBALLERS OF ALL TIME. HE WON ALL THE MAJOR PRIZES AS A PLAYER IN CLUB AND INTERNATIONAL FOOTBALL AND THEN BECAME A HIGHLY SUCCESSFUL MANAGER.

Zidane was born in Marseille in 1972 to Algerian parents who emigrated to France in the 1950s. He grew up in the deprived neighbourhood of La Castelane but never forgot his Arab roots.

Affectionately known as 'Zizou', Zidane was the inspiration for France when the team won the World Cup on home soil in 1998. In the final against Brazil, he scored two of France's three goals. After the victory, his image was beamed onto the famous Paris landmark, the Arc de Triomphe – it was a powerful symbol of a multiracial country.

Zinedine
ZIDANE

Following the end of his playing career, Zidane went into fooball management. As head coach of Real Madrid, he went on to win the Champions League three more times. As well as his many prizes in football, he was given one of France's highest awards, the *Légion d'Honneur*, which is rather like a knighthood. He remains a role model for France's many immigrant communities.

A stylish attacking midfielder, Zidane played for Juventus in Italy and for the Spanish giants Real Madrid. His winning goal for Real Madrid against Bayer Leverkusen in the 2002 Champions League final is regularly voted among the greatest in the competition. As the ball dropped out of the night sky to Zidane on the edge of the penalty area, he pirouetted like a ballet dancer and volleyed it into the top corner of the net.

Shockingly, Zidane's playing career ended in scandal when he was sent off during the 2006 World Cup final between France and Italy. He headbutted an opponent, Marco Materrazi, who is alleged to have made a racist remark towards him.

Zinédine Zidane at the *Légion d'Honneur* awards ceremony in 1998 with the then France president Jacques Chirac.

Why I'm A...
CHAMPION OF CHANGE

★ **Name:** Rhian Brewster

‼ **Age:** 22

⚽ **Favourite footballer:**
Thierry Henry

📍 **Occupation:** Professional
footballer

I have a Bajan (from Barbados) father and a Turkish Cypriot mum. Coming from a diverse background might seem weird for some people, but to me it's normal. I get to see two different cultures and that unique perspective makes me feel lucky.

I'm proud of my colour and proud to be English. Being black makes things harder but it's good to be able to speak freely about how I feel about my background. I'm from east London, but I moved to Liverpool and then to Sheffield United. It was hard moving away at a young age.

I try to be the best role model I can, both on and off the pitch. It's nice to think that young fans look up to me, but that comes with a responsibility. If I am doing something bad, they might think they can do it too.

Thierry Henry is one of my role models. On the pitch he would do stuff out of the blue. He'd just get the ball and make it look easy. I try to play like him.

I've been asked whether things have changed since we started taking the knee before games. The gesture had an initial impact but not so much now. There is still racism happening now – in football and in the everyday world. You go on social media sometimes, maybe after losing a game and all you see are monkeys or banana emojis or "black this" and "black that".

> *You go on social media sometimes, maybe after losing a game...*

> *and all you see are monkeys or banana emojis...*

We can speak out because we have a platform to do so. In everyday life, racism still happens. It happens to me. I don't want to go into too much detail, but stuff happens and you can't escape it. I want there to be more education about it, even for the older generation. Sometimes, they don't know how racially offensive a comment or an opinion might be and if they are feeding it to their children, these views will never go away. In fact, we might have to start with the older generation.

> *It's nice to think that young fans look up to me.*

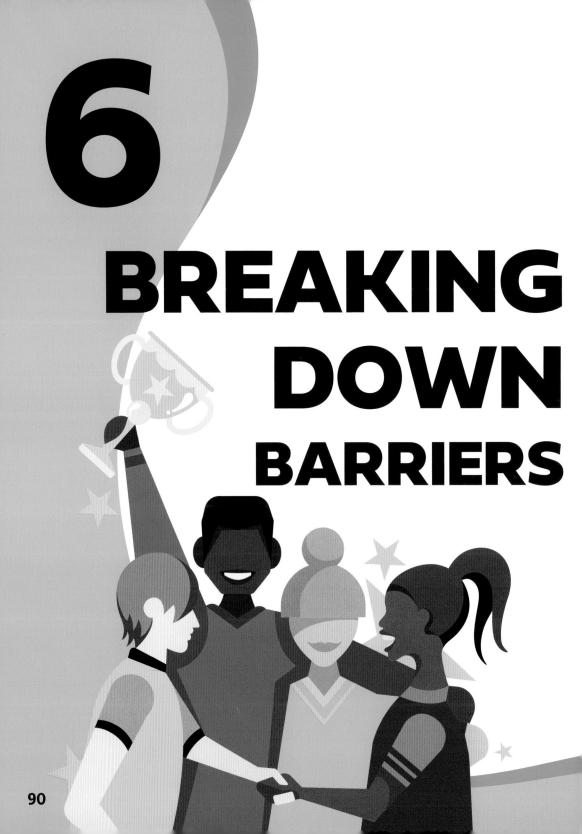

6

BREAKING DOWN BARRIERS

By 2010, the Premier League and its players had turned English football into 'The Greatest Show on Earth' – a far cry from all the hooliganism and violence that marred the sport in the 1970s and 1980s. Now, with star players from every continent, the league's global appeal reached another level.

Notably, the first British Asian players appeared in the Premier League. What's more, during this era, the profile of the women's game had grown too and became fully professional. There were iconic ethnic minority players gracing the women's game, and Dutch football legend Ruud Gullit became the first black manager in the Premier League. This was a positive start and set the scene for the English game to become truly representative on the pitch.

Diversity On The Pitch

The early trailblazers of English football, such as Arthur Wharton, Emma Clarke and Hassan Hegazi, would not recognise the modern game. Today, England has the most cosmopolitan league in the world.

On the first weekend of the Premier League, in August 1992, there were just 13 overseas players in action. Since then, players from over 100 nations have featured. A third of all players are now black and the League claims that 19 per cent of those who attend matches are from ethnic minority backgrounds.

Gunners go global

North London club Arsenal has always attracted fans from the diverse neighbourhoods surrounding its stadium. Inner-city areas, such as the boroughs of Hackney and Islington, have an ethnically diverse population.

As a wealthy club, Arsenal was able to attract the best players. Notably, former manager Arsene Wenger signed several of the France squad that won the 1998 World Cup and Euro 2000. Many, such as Thierry Henry, Patrick Vieira and Sylvain Wiltord, were black.

As a result, the team's diversity has often reflected the area it represents. The presence of so many ethnic minority players also increased the club's appeal in Africa, Asia and beyond.

In September 2002, Arsenal notched up their 22nd consecutive away win at Leeds, though the match is also remembered because the team's line-up included nine black players.

Despite the rich variety in the Premier League, there are still communities that remain under-represented in English football. The FA is committed to creating a game that is free from discrimination at all levels, but some ethnic groups still feel that football fails to provide a welcoming environment for them.

> ❝ We were living in our time. It's just that people didn't realise that's how England is. It's mixed! ❞
>
> Thierry Henry, former Arsenal striker

ALL-INCLUSIVE ENGLAND

In the summer of 1996, when England hosted the Euros, just two of the national team's players – from a 22-man squad – came from a ethnic minority background. They were Paul Ince and Sol Campbell, who helped England to reach the semi-finals.

Fast forward 16 years to Euro 2012 and that figure had skyrocketed to 50 per cent. Glen Johnson, Ashley Cole, Joleon Lescott, Ashley Young, Danny Welbeck, Alex Oxlade-Chamberlain, Jermain Defoe and Theo Walcott all represented England at the tournament held in Poland and Ukraine.

The Asian Absence

It has been a burning question for three decades: football is hugely popular among Britain's South Asian communities so why have so few Asian players made it professionally?

Jimmy Carter was the first to appear in the Premier League when he made his 1992 debut for Arsenal. His father was from India, though his surname came from an English ancestor. Carter's impact as a trailblazer among South Asian communities may have been reduced, though, because his English name and light skin tone meant that most fans were largely unaware of his South Asian heritage.

However, the statistics paint a poor picture of the British Asian presence in the game. During the 2020/21 season, out of a total of 4,000 footballers, only eight were British Asian players who made first-team appearances in England's top four divisions. By 2021, only four more home-grown South Asian players – **Neil Taylor**, **Michael Chopra**, **Hamza Choudhury** and **Zesh Rehman** – had played in the Premier League.

Jimmy Carter made 29 appearances for Arsenal between 1991 and 1995.

Out of touch

In their book *Corner Flags And Corner Shops,* Jas Bains and Sanjiev Johal point out that there is mass participation in football at amateur level among Britain's South Asian communities. However, players from those communities face huge barriers when trying to enter the professional game.

Asians who have tried to join football clubs often report being met with racist attitudes. For example, some coaches still assume that Asians make good cricketers but not good footballers, plus there's football's lack of willingness to adapt to the different needs of players, such as needs around praying and fasting. In 2020, the FA chairman Greg Clarke was forced to resign after making a series of offensive gaffes to members of Parliament. His remark about British South Asians choosing careers in IT over sport, revealed how out of touch he was.

THE ASIAN X FACTOR

The Premier League and Kick It Out launched the South Asian Action Plan in 2022. Its aim is to attract more British Asian players into professional football academies. Open auditions are held around the country that allow children between the ages of eight and 12 to showcase their footballing talents in front of academy managers and coaches. It is a brilliant opportunity for youngsters from South Asian communities to get noticed by the gatekeepers of the professional game. The successful ones get to hear the coaches say, "It's a yes from me!"

> **66** *I guess the better I do, the bigger the pathway for South Asian football.* **99**

HAMZA CHALLENGES ATTITUDES

Hamza Choudhury became an iconic figure for Britain's South Asian community as part of the Leicester City team that won the FA Cup in 2021. His mother is Bangladeshi and his father is from Grenada, in the Caribbean. A tough-tackling midfielder, Choudhury shows that stereotypes about Asian players avoiding physical contact sports are not true.

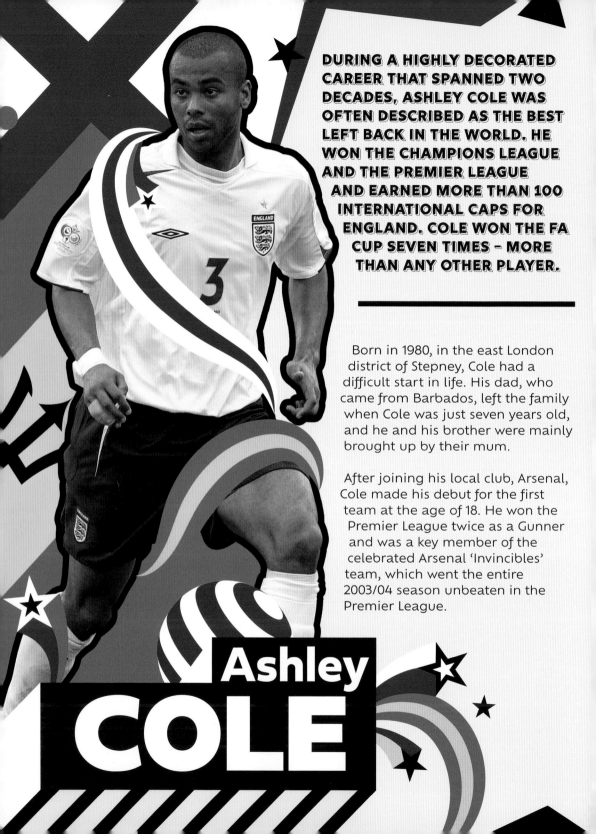

DURING A HIGHLY DECORATED CAREER THAT SPANNED TWO DECADES, ASHLEY COLE WAS OFTEN DESCRIBED AS THE BEST LEFT BACK IN THE WORLD. HE WON THE CHAMPIONS LEAGUE AND THE PREMIER LEAGUE AND EARNED MORE THAN 100 INTERNATIONAL CAPS FOR ENGLAND. COLE WON THE FA CUP SEVEN TIMES – MORE THAN ANY OTHER PLAYER.

Born in 1980, in the east London district of Stepney, Cole had a difficult start in life. His dad, who came from Barbados, left the family when Cole was just seven years old, and he and his brother were mainly brought up by their mum.

After joining his local club, Arsenal, Cole made his debut for the first team at the age of 18. He won the Premier League twice as a Gunner and was a key member of the celebrated Arsenal 'Invincibles' team, which went the entire 2003/04 season unbeaten in the Premier League.

Ashley
COLE

In 2004, while on international duty, Cole and his team-mate Shaun Wright-Phillips were targeted by Spanish football supporters making monkey noises. The Spanish Football Association was fined £45,000 for the incident.

Cole married the pop singer Cheryl Tweedy from the hugely successful group Girls Aloud in 2006 – though they divorced four years later. Soon after their wedding, Cole signed for Chelsea and won another Premier League title and the Champions League.

The star's tough upbringing on a London council estate shaped Cole as a player who was prepared to fight for everything on the pitch. Believing he received unfair press coverage over his contract negotiations and personal relationships, he felt he had to work a little bit harder than his white team-mates.

Ashley Cole thrived on marking the world's best players, such as Cristiano Ronaldo.

❝ I just said to myself I am going to work as hard as I can and not let anyone have that hold over me. ❞

Cole in an interview with Sky Sports in 2020

Cole is not put off by the fact that there are so few black managers in football. He has worked as a coach for Chelsea's Academy and the England Under 21 team. Appointed as a member of Everton's coaching staff in 2022, he is determined to one day become a manager in England's top league.

As a brilliant attacking left back, Cole won 107 caps for England and played in three World Cups. The legendary Portugal striker Cristiano Ronaldo, who was often marked by Cole when their teams met, once admitted that Cole was his toughest opponent.

The Women's Game Takes Off

England's Lionesses captured the hearts of the nation in the Women's Euro 2022 championship. They beat Germany 2–1 in the final, capping of a brilliant tournament. Record numbers watched the Lionesses lift England's first major trophy in 56 years.

It was not the first time the women's game had drawn huge crowds. In the early part of the 20th century, the game was thriving – in 1920, a match at Everton's home ground, Goodison Park, drew a crowd of 53,000. Less than a year later, the FA banned women from playing matches in stadiums, effectively banning elite women's football because the sport was 'unsuitable' for females. That ban lasted for nearly 50 years – and it was not until 1993 that the women's game was brought under the control of the FA.

Diversity firsts

The Women's Football Association was formed in 1969, but it wasn't until 1982 that the first ethnic minority player represented England. **Kerry Davis** made her debut against Northern Ireland, scoring two goals. She went on to make 82 appearances and scored 44 goals during her 16-year international career.

In 2003, **Mary Phillip** became the first black woman to captain the England team – 10 years after Paul Ince had achieved the honour with the men's side. She played 65 times for the national team before retiring in 2008. Today, she is the manager of Peckham Town in the men's Kent County league.

"FRESH & FUNNY. THIS IS THE
BEST BRITISH COMEDY
SINCE BRIDGET JONES'S DIARY."

A FILM BY GURINDER CHADHA

LIKE BEC

Who wants to cook
when you can bend a

NAMRATA
NAGRA   KN

BEND IT LIKE BECKHAM

This 2002 box-office smash hit tells the story of a British-Indian teenager whose family refuses to support her passion for football. Jess Bhamra plays for a local women's team without her parents' permission – her dad fears she may face the same racial prejudice he experienced in cricket.

The most successful football film of all time, *Bend It Like Beckham* cast a spotlight on the representation of women in football, challenged stereotypes about South Asian women being unsuited to playing and proved inspirational for many women in sport.

AMAZING ALUKO

Born in Nigeria in 1987, Eniola Aluko moved to Birmingham with her parents when she was still a baby. Joining the England squad at 14, she enjoyed stellar career in England, Italy and the USA, scoring 33 goals in 102 international appearances.

Aluko accused the former England coach Mark Sampson of making racist comments to her and a team-mate in 2014. She received an apology from Sampson and was paid compensation by the FA.

In 2014, Aluko became the first female pundit on the BBC's Match Of The Day. Since retiring as a player, she has worked as a director of women's football for Aston Villa and the Women's Soccer League in the United States.

All-White England

Although the Lionesses' victory at Euro 2022 was a milestone for the women's game, the tournament also shone a light on a glaring lack of diversity in England's team.

Just three ethnic minority players – Demi Stokes, Nikita Parris and Jess Carter – were in the squad. None of them started a game, playing just 20 minutes of football between them during the entire tournament. In contrast, France – who reached the quarter-finals – featured 15 ethnic minority players in their 23-woman squad. Perhaps, more tellingly, the England men's team had 11 black or mixed-race players for their European Championship just a year earlier, accounting for almost half of the 23-men squad. Surely the England women's squad should be more diverse and comparable to that of the men's?

The Lionnesses line up for a team photo ahead of the team's match against Norway at Euro 2022.

Scouting for talent

So, why isn't there more diversity in the women's team? Currently, there are fewer than 30 black, Asian or mixed-heritage players at elite level in the Women's Super League.

One possible reason is that talent scouts may not be looking in the right places for women and girls from diverse backgrounds. The WSL Academies are often situated in wealthy suburbs with mainly white, middle-class populations. Traditionally, there has been less money in the women's game – and that means there is less funding available to help talented ethnic minority youngsters from the inner cities to travel safely to academies.

Some ethnic groups also face barriers in their own communities when taking up an activity. In certain cultures, girls and women playing football is discouraged.

SEE IT, ACHIEVE IT

Recognising the lack of visible role models from diverse ethnic backgrounds, the Professional Footballers' Association launched the See It, Achieve It. campaign to inspire the next generation of players. If youngsters can see other female players from similar backgrounds to them, they can find heroes to emulate.

Meanwhile, England Football's Discover My Talent project and Emerging Talent Centres promise to look harder for the best female players from different backgrounds and create a more diverse-looking England side in the future.

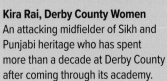

Kira Rai, Derby County Women
An attacking midfielder of Sikh and Punjabi heritage who has spent more than a decade at Derby County after coming through its academy.

Simran Jhamat, Coventry United
Another flag-bearer for British South Asian women who also played as a striker for Liverpool, Leicester and Bristol City.

Layla Banaras, Birmingham City
A great future England prospect in her club's academy, who admits she has not seen many Muslim or Asian girls playing.

A TRAILBLAZING FORMER ENGLAND INTERNATIONAL AND ARSENAL LEGEND, ALEX SCOTT'S CAREER HIGHLIGHTS INCLUDE SCORING THE WINNING GOAL FOR ARSENAL IN THE FINAL OF THE 2007 UEFA WOMEN'S CUP. SHE WAS INDUCTED INTO THE FOOTBALL HALL OF FAME IN 2019 AND HAS SINCE BECOME A TOP TV PRESENTER.

When Scott was a child, she recalls her mum, Carol McKee, as her ultimate role model, who taught Scott how to be strong and the value of hard work.

A chance meeting with an Arsenal talent scout put Scott on the road to stardom. She was the only girl playing cage football with local boys when she was spotted at the age of six. Many youngsters play this fast-paced form of the game on a mini pitch inside a metal cage.

Scott won 20 domestic trophies over three spells at Arsenal, the club she always supported. She also played in the United States for Boston Breakers.

Alex
SCOTT

The skilful defender won 140 caps for England, playing in three World Cups and five European Championships, and represented Great Britain at the 2012 London Olympics.

After retiring from playing, Scott dedicated herself to a second career in the media – working for Sky Sports and the BBC as a presenter of *The One Show* and *Football Focus*.

In 2019, she finished fifth in the *Strictly Come Dancing* TV show alongside her professional dance partner, Neil Jones. The defender-turned-dancer is a mentor to the young players in the current England Women's team and was a high-profile presenter during the Euro 2022 tournament.

On her way to becoming one of football's leading female pundits and presenters, Scott has had to confront racist and sexist comments on social media. In 2020, she shared a poem she had written in defiance of her online tormentors.

In 2019, Scott completed an 11-week streak on Strictly Come Dancing.

Off-The-Pitch Pioneers

Ethnic minority managers are shockingly under-represented in the Premier League. In its 30-year history, only 10 BAME managers have led teams in England's elite division. Here are some of the pioneers who have broken down barriers in football management.

Tony Collins

Years active: 1960–1980

Rochdale's Tony Collins was the Football League's first black manager and the first to manage at a major final, the League Cup in 1962. He became a respected scout for Leeds United, Manchester United and England.

Sammy Chung

Years active: 1976–1996

Sammy Chung was the first Asian manager in the old first division, with Wolves in 1977. Chung was of mixed Chinese and English heritage, as was Frank Soo (see page 42), who managed second-division side Scunthorpe United in 1959.

Ruud Gullit

Years active: 1996–2011

Dutch football legend Ruud Gullit was the first black manager in the Premier League, having taken over as player-manager of Chelsea in 1996. He repeated Tony Collins' feat at Rochdale by guiding Chelsea to a major cup final in 1997 – and went one better by winning!

Chris Hughton

Years active: 1997–2021

Among the most respected managers in the English game, Chris Hughton has managed three Premier League clubs – Newcastle United, Norwich City and Brighton. He was also twice caretaker manager of Tottenham Hotspur, where he had been a player.

Paul Ince

Years active: 2006–

Paul Ince became the first British-born black manager when briefly in charge of Blackburn Rovers in 2008. Ince, who was also the first black footballer to captain England, has subsequently managed MK Dons, Notts County, Blackpool and Reading.

THE ROONEY RULE

This rule has nothing to do with Wayne Rooney! It was established in American Football in 2003. The policy means that all National Football League (NFL) teams must interview a number of qualified ethnic minority candidates when choosing a new head coach, to give applicants from different backgrounds a fairer chance. Fourteen coaches from minority backgrounds were employed in the first decade, though that number has since gone down. A version of the Rooney Rule is being tried out in some areas of English football, but it may take several years to judge if it is successful.

Why I'm A...
CHAMPION
OF CHANGE

Name: Annie Zaidi

Age: 39

Favourite footballer:
Thierry Henry

Occupation:
Football Coach

People have made judgements about the way I look throughout my life, but I have never let that stop me from being who I am or what I want to be. I am proud of my faith and background. I have more trainers than high heels, and the highlight of my Saturday is watching **Match Of The Day!**

My love of football started in the back garden and eventually coaching football became my job. There has been plenty of heartache along the way, but don't feel sorry for me. I pursued this career for me and for those who look like me because equality of opportunity matters and because I matter. I fought for equal rights in a male-dominated industry. I wanted to be a coach – not a coach in the men or the women's game, just a coach. That alone has raised eyebrows!

When you tell me I can't do something, it's like a red rag to a bull and makes me even more determined. My personal motto is: "They can take away my ball, but they can't take away my passion."

When I was studying at Durham University, I took my first training session with a group of burly young men. Being just 5 feet 2 inches, I looked up at all of them and had to assert my position as coach for the next 12 weeks. I had to take the knock-downs and picked up plenty of bruises, but I was determined and within 12 weeks, they just saw me as Coach Annie.

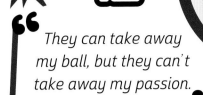

They can take away my ball, but they can't take away my passion.

I ended up being the only female manager out of hundreds in the league, but I decided to step down because of all the racist and sexist comments. One manager even refused to shake my hand at the end of a game. I knew I was worth more than that.

However, I didn't let this experience ruin my passion for the game. I have gone on to become the highest qualified Muslim female football coach in the country and I hold the coveted UEFA B Licence. I am a national ambassador for Sporting Equals, Women in Football and Football for Peace. My proudest moment has been undertaking the UEFA A Coaching qualification. The training ground is where I belong and where I can just be Coach Annie.

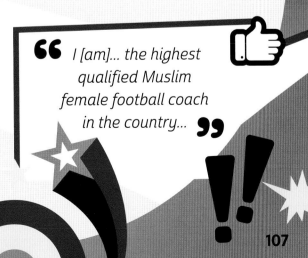

I [am]... the highest qualified Muslim female football coach in the country...

7

THE FIGHT
GOES ON...

Throughout the history of football, ethnic minority players and fans have faced abuse and discrimination because of society's ignorance and intolerance. Thanks to the work of countless pioneers and activists – many of them fans, players or former players – progress has been made to change the game for the better.

But for all the headway, there is still much more that needs to be done. Racist abuse continues to rear its ugly head in football grounds and on social media, while ethnic minority players are demanding a fairer chance of becoming coaches and managers after they stop playing. The fight goes on...

Racism In The Current Era

Today, at least a third of all players in the English Premier League are from ethnic minority backgrounds (that figure is lower in the Women's Super League, around 15 per cent in 2023).

Oi, @€*%!

??

YOU ******!

Among spectators, too, there is greater diversity than ever before. But racism remains a serious problem. A 2018 report by Kick It Out found that half of all football fans in a survey had witnessed racist abuse, and less than half knew how to report it.

Racist fans are increasingly using social media to spread their hate. This is mainly how England's black players were targeted following the final of Euro 2020 (see page 12). In one recent survey, 43 per cent of black players reported receiving racist abuse online. There has also been a significant increase in cases of Islamophobia (prejudice against Islam or Muslims) and anti-semitism (hostility against Jewish people).

Players at war

Sadly, racism has been known to erupt on the pitch too. In 2012, John Terry, the former Chelsea and England captain, was involved in a high-profile court case after being accused of hurling a racial insult at QPR's Anton Ferdinand. Terry was cleared in court, but he was fined and given a four-match ban by the Football Association.

During a match in 2011, Liverpool's Luis Suárez used an outdated and offensive word for a black person during a confrontation with Patrice Evra of Manchester United. Suárez was banned for eight matches.

In 2015, the Premier League and Kick It Out joined forces to tackle the issue of racism on the pitch. Many professional

players were already being taught about the importance of respecting people from all backgrounds. Now the scheme has been extended to young academy footballers with the hope that future first-team players would avoid repeating the shameful episodes of the past.

A NIGHT OF SHAME

In 2019, one of the most appalling nights in football unfolded during England's Euro qualifier against Bulgaria, held in the country's capital city, Sofia. While the noise of monkey chants and images of the home fans performing Nazi salutes were broadcast globally, play was stopped twice and the match came close to being abandoned.

The Bulgarian crowd had already been reduced in size as a punishment for previous racist behaviour. Now, UEFA ordered Bulgaria to play one match without any fans at all and fined them £70,000. However, anti-racism campaigners said the punishment didn't go far enough. UEFA have since appointed former footballers Bobby Barnes and Célia Šašić as the first black members of its Control, Ethics and Disciplinary body. They say they will take a much stricter approach to racist incidents in the game.

Unfairness At The Top

Many managers and coaches used to be pro footballers, so given that we now see a diversity on the pitch, why are nearly all managers white?

About a quarter of the players in the 92 elite English clubs are non-white, but there have only been 10 non-white managers in the Premier League to date.

Plenty of ethnic minority players study to get the right coaching qualifications only to discover that no club wants to give them a job or even an interview. Many of them give up on their ambitions of becoming a manager or look abroad to find work.

The former Netherlands striker Jimmy Floyd Hasselbaink has managed three Football League clubs. He believes many black coaches simply do not bother getting their qualifications because they do not expect to find opportunities.

However, gaining the right qualifications might have little bearing on getting a job in top-flight football. Recruiting a new manager may not happen in a formal way and owners often rely on their own private network

> “I do think that people look at black managers or coaches in a different way.”
>
> Jimmy Floyd Hasselbaink speaking to Sky Sports

of contacts to select a coach – ethnic minority candidates may not be part of these groups.

It's also possible that bosses are showing unconscious bias (see page 18) by making unfair assumptions about ethnic minority applicants. For example, they might assume non-white candidates make good players but lack the deeper understanding of the game required to be effective managers.

Words matter

In 2020, a group of researchers investigating unconscious racial bias in football commentary made a remarkable discovery. Players with a lighter skin tone received far more praise for their intelligence and hard work than those with darker skin – who were more likely to be praised for athletic qualities such as pace and power. This reinforces a popular stereotype that black athletes are less intelligent and only succeed because of their natural physical ability.

These kinds of descriptions count against non-white footballers. Players who are regularly described as intelligent and hard-working have an unfair advantage when applying for jobs in management.

URIAH RENNIE

In a career that lasted nearly 30 years, Uriah Rennie – the first and only black referee to officiate in the Premier League – took charge of more than 170 matches. Unfortunately, his success has not led to greater diversity among match officials. In 2021, out of around 200 refereees in the top seven divisions of English football, only four were black or Asian. Since hanging up his whistle in 2008, Rennie has campaigned for greater equality of opportunity for ethnic minority referees.

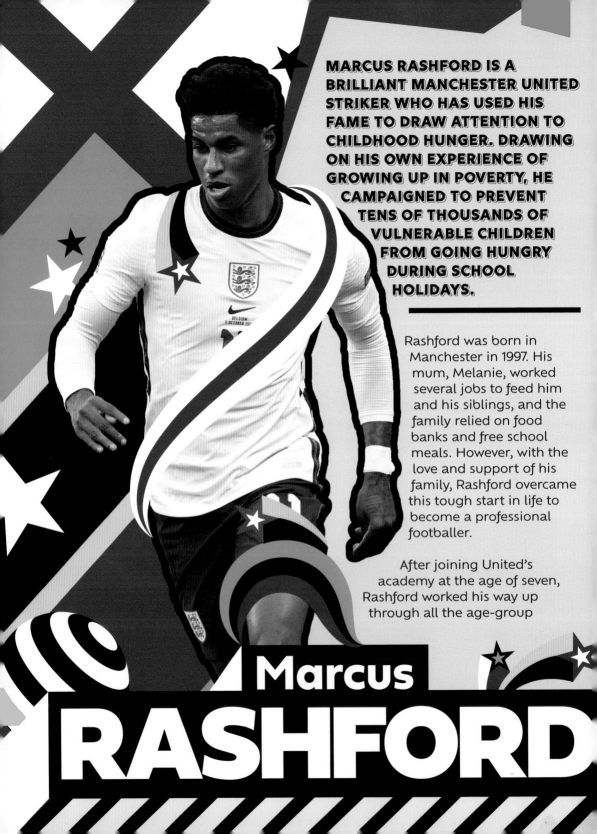

MARCUS RASHFORD IS A BRILLIANT MANCHESTER UNITED STRIKER WHO HAS USED HIS FAME TO DRAW ATTENTION TO CHILDHOOD HUNGER. DRAWING ON HIS OWN EXPERIENCE OF GROWING UP IN POVERTY, HE CAMPAIGNED TO PREVENT TENS OF THOUSANDS OF VULNERABLE CHILDREN FROM GOING HUNGRY DURING SCHOOL HOLIDAYS.

Rashford was born in Manchester in 1997. His mum, Melanie, worked several jobs to feed him and his siblings, and the family relied on food banks and free school meals. However, with the love and support of his family, Rashford overcame this tough start in life to become a professional footballer.

After joining United's academy at the age of seven, Rashford worked his way up through all the age-group

Marcus
RASHFORD

teams, scoring goals and building up his strength and stamina. He got his big breakthrough when he was just 18. Making a sensational Premier League debut, he scored two goals in a 3–2 win against Arsenal. A few months later, the striker also scored in his first appearance for the senior England team in a victory over Australia.

The Manchester United star has won the FA Cup, the League Cup and the Europa League for his club, and represented England in the World Cup twice and in the Euros. But Rashford is just as famous for backing campaigns in support of greater equality as he is for dazzling football.

> **66** These children matter and as long as they don't have a voice, they will have mine. **99**
>
> Marcus Rashford

In March 2020, during the first Covid-19 lockdown, Rashford joined forces with the FareShare charity to help raise money for children who were no longer receiving free school meals. He has helped raise millions of pounds in donations from supermarkets.

In June of that year, Rashford called for an end to child poverty, persuading the government to provide Britain's poorest children with free meals during the school holidays.

Rashford is also a passionate supporter of anti-racism campaigns, particularly after experiencing racial abuse at Euro 2020. In 2021, he was among a

One of the many messages of support Rashford received following Euro 2020.

number of footballers who joined Hope United, a group set up by BT to tackle online hate. He appeared in its film encouraging children to read books to help them understand black history and culture.

In 2021, Rashford received an MBE from Prince William, in recognition of his work to support vulnerable children. He dedicated the award to his mum and has vowed to keep campaigning to lift children out of poverty.

Rashford has been an ambassador of FareShare since March 2020.

No To Racism

Fans sitting down to watch England's friendly against Switzerland on Sky TV in September 2018 were in for a surprise. The first 25 seconds of the match were shown in black and white. It was a clever device to mark the 25th anniversary of Kick It Out.

The battle against racism in football has come a long way in that time. The hard work of organisations such as Kick It Out and Show Racism the Red Card – which also celebrated its 25th birthday more recently – has forced football to confront discrimination in the game. Those organisations have spoken out consistently on the issue and educated thousands of people about it along the way.

> **❝**I look back on the last 25 years with a sense of paternal pride at how far we have come.**❞**
>
> Shaka Hislop, Honorary President of Show Racism the Red Card and former Newcastle United goalkeeper

Taking the knee

The gesture of 'taking the knee' can be traced back to American football player Colin Kaepernick, a quarterback for the San Francisco 49ers. In 2016, he began to kneel before games during the national anthem as a protest against racial injustice and police brutality – in the USA, police are much more likely to shoot and kill unarmed African Americans than white people, and these shootings often go unpunished. By taking the knee, Kaepernick started an important debate in the country about racial inequality.

Colin Kaepernick (left) taking the knee with a team-mate

Following the murder of African American George Floyd by a white policeman in 2020, Premier League players and managers also began to 'take the knee' before their matches – and England's players continued to do so during Euro 2020. Although some politicians saw it as creating division, England's manager, Gareth Southgate, explained that it was not a political gesture but a way for players to show solidarity with each other. The backlash against three black members of the team who missed penalties at Euro 2020 (see page 12) showed the importance of taking the knee to oppose racism.

I CAN'T BREATHE!

In 2020, African American George Floyd was murdered by a police officer in the US city of Minneapolis. Under arrest for the suspected use of counterfeit money in a shop, Floyd died when the police officer knelt on his neck. The horrifying incident was captured on video and Floyd's words, *"I can't breathe"*, became a powerful slogan associated with the **Black Lives Matter** movement. The brutality of his murder sent shockwaves around the world and inspired a global campaign for racial equality.

The Power of Social Media

As the experience of some of England's black players during Euro 2020 revealed, one of the biggest battlegrounds in the fight against racism in football is social media.

An independent report released by FIFA showed that more than half the players who featured in Euro 2020 and the Africa Cup of Nations in 2022 were abused online – and 38 per cent of those messages were found to be racist in nature.

The problem of online trolling is a difficult one to police since social media platforms are places where abusers can easily hide.

66 [they can] throw a digital banana at someone on Twitter with virtually no consequences. **99**

Sanjay Bhandari, chairman of Kick It Out

Taking on the trolls

Footballers are demanding that tech companies do more to stop online trolls, and the UK government has threatened these firms with large fines if they do not act.

The companies are developing new technology to filter out abusive messages so they cannot be seen by their intended target or their followers. Some have taken down thousands of football-related tweets that break the rules.

However, many feel the tech companies haven't gone far enough. In 2021, former Arsenal striker **Thierry Henry** quit social media, in protest against the lack of action by company owners to stop online harassment: "The sheer volume of racism, bullying and resulting mental torture is too toxic to ignore."

He was one of several former and current footballers to speak out on the issue. It led the UK government to announce plans for a change in the law, extending football banning orders to those who are abusive online.

SOCIAL MEDIA BOYCOTT

For four days in the spring of 2021, football had nothing to do with social media. Rugby, cricket, netball and Formula One all took part in this boycott to highlight the need for more to be done to tackle the problem of online abuse.

> 66 We are switching off our social media channels from 3pm on Friday 30 April until 23:59pm on Monday 3 May, in response to sustained and ongoing online abuse. 99
>
> Raheem Sterling

#ENOUGH

#StopOnlineAbuse

Hope, Not Hate

In the past, players who suffered racial abuse often felt frightened and alone. Of course, this can still be the case – but although social media has made footballers an easy target for racists, it has also given them an effective means of fighting back.

Social media platforms are different from traditional media. In newspapers and magazines, for example, comments are selected by others before being published, but social media users are able to control the message they send to their followers.

High-profile footballers such as **Marcus Rashford** (see pages 114–115) and **Son Heung-Min** attract millions of followers on social media. They and many others are able to use it to express their opinions on all sorts of subjects.

Of course, football supporters can also experience racial hatred and harassment on social media. However, it can also be a safe space to report incidents of abuse or to connect with others fighting for change.

THE SALAH EFFECT

Liverpool's Mohamed 'Mo' Salah has over 50 million followers on Instagram and uses his star profile to fight racial discrimination. The Egypt international celebrates goals by falling to his knees and saying a prayer. He has been a victim of Islamophobia, but the footballer isn't afraid to speak out against such abuse.

A study by Stanford University in the USA revealed the dramatic effect Salah's performances have had on crime levels in Liverpool. It found that following his arrival at the club, hate crime in the city fell by 19 per cent, and online anti-Muslim comments also reduced by half.

> **"** There's no place for racism in football. There's no place for racism anywhere at all. **"**
>
> Mohamed Salah on Twitter, December 2018

NO ROOM FOR RACISM

Although racism in football has not gone away – a poll by Ipsos in 2022 revealed that almost two thirds of fans in Britain believe it remains a problem – the game has certainly come a long way since early pioneers like Arthur Wharton first proved their skill with the ball.

Stars such as **Raheem Sterling** (see pages 16–17) and **Marcus Rashford** have shown how football can have a positive impact on society. It can be a spearhead in creating further equality for all, regardless of race or ethnicity. For progress to continue, those running football need to create a more diverse workforce and heed the voices of black former players.

Why I'm A...
CHAMPION
OF CHANGE

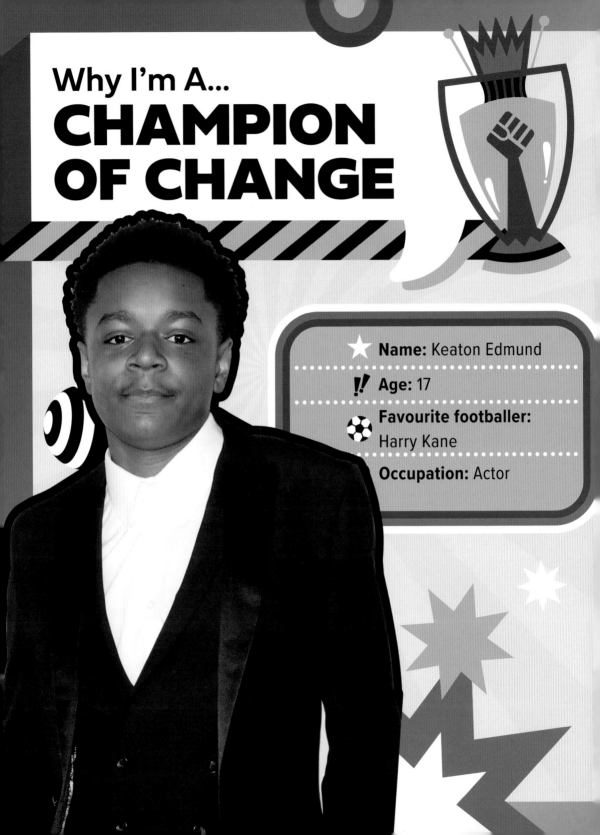

★ **Name:** Keaton Edmund

‼ **Age:** 17

⚽ **Favourite footballer:**
Harry Kane

Occupation: Actor

My name is Keaton and I play Freddie in the CBBC show *Jamie Johnson*. It was nerve-racking when I found out that the show was covering a storyline in which my character would face racism on a football pitch. I had to show the audience what Freddie was going through so my acting had to be convincing.

The episode was filmed just after the EURO 2020 final when Bukayo Saka, Marcus Rashford and Jadon Sancho received racist abuse after their penalty misses (see page 12). I was proud to take on the storyline – in which our team has to decide in the changing room whether to abandon the match in support of my character or continue playing. The hardest thing for my character, Freddie, was calling out the situation. He could have easily just carried on playing, kept it inside and told no one else. But he made a stand and I think the team did the right thing by coming off the pitch.

The scene in the changing room was hard to film. We filmed for two days in just that one spot. It turned out well so was worth it. When you experience something negative – it can be racism or any form of discrimination – you need to know that you are not alone. Your team-mates should always support you. If they don't then you know that's not the place for you.

When I first saw players taking the knee – I think it was in one of the England games – I thought it was a good gesture. In one of the episodes of *Jamie Johnson,* we actually took the knee as well – inspired by the professional players. It's grass roots football but it has an effect across all levels of football, all sports and everyone watching. There are loads of people who watch football.

> " *When you experience something negative – it can be racism or any form of discrimination* "

> " *– you need to know that you are not alone.* "

Stamping Out Racism In Football

1881
Andrew Watson becomes the first black international footballer and captains Scotland to a 6–1 victory against England on his debut.

1909
Walter Tull becomes England's first black professional outfield player when he turns out for Tottenham Hotspur in a 3–1 defeat at Sunderland.

1931
Eddie Parris is the first black footballer to represent Wales when he makes his first and only international appearance against Ireland in Belfast.

1933
Stoke City's **Frank Soo** becomes the first player of Chinese heritage to appear in the Football League and later for England in unofficial wartime internationals.

1991
The UK parliament introduces **The Football Offences Act**, which bans indecent and racist chants, pitch invasions and the throwing of missiles at football matches.

1993
The charity **Kick It Out** is launched to tackle racism in football. (It will later expand its remit to fight all forms of discrimination in football.)

1999
The **FARE network** is set up to counter discrimination in European football after a meeting of players and supporters' groups in Vienna.

1889

Goalkeeper **Arthur Wharton** joins Rotherham Town as the first black professional footballer and is the first to play in the Football League.

1895

Emma Clarke makes her debut for the British Ladies' Football Club and becomes the first black professional female player in Britain.

1901

Willie Clarke is the first non-white professional footballer to score in the English first division with a goal for Aston Villa against Everton, on Christmas Day.

1970

Brazil win the first World Cup broadcast in colour with a multi-ethnic team playing football that takes the game to new heights.

1978

Viv Anderson is the first black footballer to appear for the senior men's England national team, in his debut against Czechoslovakia.

1990

England name three black players – **Paul Parker, Des Walker and John Barnes** – in their starting line-up for the first time, at the World Cup finals in Italy.

2013

AC Milan's **Kevin-Prince Boateng** walks off the pitch after racist abuse and later becomes an ambassador for FIFA's anti-discrimination task force.

2016

The English Football League pilots the 'Rooney Rule' to ensure clubs interview at least one non-white candidate for managerial vacancies.

2022

The Premier League launches its South Asian Action Plan to increase the numbers of British South Asian players in football academies.

Index

Acknowledgements

The author would like to thank the following for their contribution towards making this book happen:

Suhel Ahmed
Carl Anka, *The Athletic*
Stella Caldwell
Kevin Cookson, *Sheffield United*
Brian Deane
Ruth Johnson, *Football Unites Racism Divides*
Emma Norris, *Manchester City*
Troy Townsend, *Kick It Out*
Mark Thomas
The Daily Mail newspaper
The Guardian newspaper

The publishers would like to thank the following sources for their kind permission to reproduce the pictures in this book. (T-top, B-bottom, L-left, R-right)

ALAMY: Action Foto Sport 101C; agefotostock 34L; Allstar Picture Library Ltd 96, 102; Artokoloro 19; Jason Cairnduff/Action Images/Reuters 105R; Simon Dack / Telephoto Images 41B; Granger; Historical Picture Archive 29; Howard Harrison 13; Andrew Hasson 105C; Historic Collection 32; Moviestore Collection Ltd 99R; News Images Ltd 121; PA Images 73, 74, 76, 86, 105L, 113B; Mark Pain 79B; RBM Vintage Images 43T; Carl Recine/Reuters 16; Reuters 75; SPP Sport Press Photo 101L; Trinity Mirror/Mirrorpix 62, 63B, 70; Mick Sinclair 65TR; Lia Toby/BAFTA 122; Mark Waugh 115B; Jason Wells 15BR; Zuma Press 101R

STUART BOULTON: 33

COLORSPORT: 104L

FURD: Kevin Titterton 79T

GETTY IMAGES: Gerry Armes/Birmingham Mail/Popperfoto 104R; Matthew Ashton/AMA 116BR; Naomi Baker 103T; Robbie Jay Barratt/AMA 82; James Baylis/AMA 99L; Martin Bernetti/AFP 81L; Bettmann 61R; Lynne Cameron/The FA 36, 98; David Cannon/Allsport 63T, 64R; Daily Mirror/Mirrorpix 56; David Davies/Offside 6; Danilo Di Giovanni/The FA 88; Paul Ellis/AFP 116BL, 119; Craig Foy/SNS Group 115T; Tom Jenkins 8; Jan Kruger 116L; Eileen Langsley/Popperfoto 47R; Pascal Le Segretain/FIFA 15BC; Christian Liewig/TempSport/Corbis 87; Liverpool FC 65BR; Stuart MacFarlane/Arsenal FC 15BL; Richard Martin-Roberts/CameraSport 81R; Stephanie Meek/CameraSport 100; Mirror Group Newspapers/Mirrorpix 58; Steve Morton/Allsport 94; Katja Ogrin/Redferns 103B; Valerio Pennicino 20; Alberto Pizzoli/AFP 83; Popperfoto 55T; Peter Powell 80; The Print Collector 30; Tom Purslow/Manchester United 97; Duncan Raban/Popperfoto 64L; Michael Regan/AFP 114; Helen H. Richardson/MediaNews Group/The Denver Post 117B; Rolfo 113T; Rolls Press/Popperfoto 54; Jeff Spicer/Premier League 77; Bob Thomas/Popperfoto 35T, 35R, 40, 43B; Bob Thomas Sports Photography 21, 47L, 55B, 61L; Topical Press Agency 44; Christian Verheyen/Borussia Moenchengladbach 81C; Visionhaus 95; Andrew Yates/AFP 111; Michael Zagaris/San Francisco 49ers 117T

SHUTTERSTOCK: ANL 42; Colorsport 48; Monty Fresco/Daily Mail 45

UNIVERSITY OF WARWICK: (Dazzler socks racists) ; Leamington Anti-Racist, Anti-Fascist Committee archive, Modern Records Centre, University of Warwick (MSS.247/11) 65TL

WEST HAM UNITED FC: 59

WIKIMEDIA COMMONS: 34R, 35L

Every effort has been made to acknowledge correctly and contact the source and/or copyright holder of each picture. Any unintentional errors or omissions will be corrected in future editions of this book.